Lost Souls: FOUND! ™

Inspirational Stories of Adopted Boston Terriers

Kyla Duffy and Lowrey Mumford

Published by Happy Tails Books™, LLC

Happy Tails Books™ publishes breed-specific compilations of stories about rescued dogs. These thought-provoking books are meant to entertain pet lovers and raise awareness about pet adoption and typical characteristics of the breed at hand. They provide a venue for proud owners to showcase their adopted pets and generate funding for rescue groups through the donation of a portion of each sale.

Lost Souls: Found! ™

Inspirational Stories of Adopted Boston Terriers by Kyla Duffy and Lowrey Mumford

Published by Happy Tails Books™, LLC   www.happytailsbooks.com

The publisher gratefully acknowledges the numerous Boston Terrier rescue groups and their members who generously granted permission to use their stories and photos.

Front cover photo: "Mickey" courtesy of Morgan Miller.   www.cornerstonephotography.com

Back cover and interior photos (that are not associated with a specific story): "Chloe" courtesy of April Ziegler.

www.aprilziegler.com

Publishers Cataloging In Publication

Lost Souls: Found!™ Inspirational Stories of Adopted Boston Terriers/ [Compiled and edited by] Kyla Duffy and Lowrey Mumford.

p. ; cm.

ISBN: 978-0-9824895-0-5

1. Boston terrier. 2. Dog rescue. 3. Dogs – Anecdotes. 4. Animal welfare – United States. 5. Human-animal relationships – Anecdotes. I. Duffy, Kyla. II. Mumford, Lowrey. III. Title.

SF426.5   2010

636.72-dc21   2009904945

Thank you to the following groups, who helped us collect stories for this book:

Arizona Boston Terrier Rescue
http://www.azbtrescue.org/

Boston Terrier Rescue of North Carolina
http://www.btrnc.org/

Bostons by the Bay
http://www.bostonsbythebay.com/

Friends of Homeless Animals
http://members.petfinder.com/~RI76/

MidAmerica Boston Terrier Rescue
http://www.adoptaboston.com/

Midwest Boston Terrier Rescue
http://www.midwestbtrescue.org/

Northeast Boston Terrier Rescue
http://www.nebostonrescue.org/

Boston Terrier Rescue of Western Washington
http://www.btrww.org/frames.html

Southern Boston Terrier Rescue
http://www.bostonbuddies.org/

Woof!, A Boston Terrier Board
http://www.Woofboard.com/

Thank you, also, to all of the contributors whose thought-provoking stories made this book come to life!

Table of Contents

Foreword

W hile reading through some of the stories submitted for this book, I couldn't help but think about the 1950's Patti Page song, *"How Much is that Doggie in the Window?"* You know the song. It's stuck in your head now...

I can remember my excitement as a child, every time I'd approach the pet store at the mall. My mom never escaped having to suffer my, "Mommy, Mommy, they're so cute! Let's get one!" pleadings as we passed by.

I believed the doggies in the window came from a beautiful farm with manicured lawns, butterflies and rainbows. It was a place where the puppies, and their parents, were cared for and loved. A place where everyone was happy, healthy and safe.

My rosy glasses were shattered when I learned, as an adult, how contrary reality is to my idealistic vision of the perfect puppyhood. It turns out that dogs sold at commercial pet stores (like the one I was enchanted by at the mall as a child) usually do come from farms; but that is where the similarity to my vision ends. At *these* dog farms, also known as "puppy mills," the parents, or "breeders," are usually identified simply by a number, and never given a name. I won't go into too much detail as a handful of the stories herein illuminate puppy mill life; but a little background for the uninitiated might be helpful.

A puppy mill is designed solely for the cheap, mass-production of pedigree puppies. Multitudes of different dog breeds are stored in small stacked cages, often with wire floors. Dogs rarely leave these cages and human interaction is the bare minimum: food and water; coupling breeding partners; removing puppies. The females are mated every time they come into heat, and usually last no more than five years. The result is not only emotionally and physically sick parents, but ailing puppies as well.

People who run puppy mills are called "millers" not "breeders." When a dog is no longer beneficial to a miller, the lucky ones may be rescued, though unfortunately not all are "so lucky." For the ones that are, they either get put out to auction, where rescue groups can acquire them through brokers that pose as millers, or they are obtained by a special kind of volunteer who serves as a liaison between millers and rescue groups. These volunteers are trusted by the millers and frequent the mills, silently, yet sadly, passing by the dogs they cannot liberate. They know going in that they cannot save them all, and must take heart in their ability to save a few whenever possible. These brave volunteers then contact different breed-specific rescues to see if they have foster homes available.

The percentage of dogs that come into rescue from mills varies between groups. Some take in a majority of mill dogs, while others work more with strays and owner "surrenders," which occur for a variety of reasons. Often, as you may have assumed, the dog is surrendered because the owners didn't research the breed and ended up with the wrong dog for their family. Other times, however, the dog is surrendered due to an unfortunate circumstance like divorce, or the need for the owner to move into nursing care. Shelter organizations contact rescue groups when they are having a hard time placing a particular dog with a family, possibly because the dog is frightened in the shelter environment, or is passed by due to its age. Regardless of the situation, rescue groups step up to the challenge by paying for medical bills, providing foster care and securing loving forever families for these dogs in need.

These notes about mills and rescue should help you better understand the stories herein. This book is not about faulting those who have succumbed to the cute little faces staring at them eagerly through the pet store glass. It is instead a tribute to the rescue groups who have saved so many "breeders," and other wayward dogs too. They have placed these dogs with enlightened owners, who have in turn received more love and joy that they could ever have imagined.

So, how much, REALLY, is that doggie in the window? I believe you'll find, after reading these "tails," that the cost is unreasonably high. Let's work together to "bring that cost down," by supporting rescue groups and adopting wonderful, loving dogs. The doggie in the window will find a home anyway; but if we continue to educate people, eventually there will only be puppies from reputable breeders, and there will no longer be doggies in windows at all.

Kyla Duffy with assistance from Tiffany Didyk of Northeast Boston Terrier Rescue

Introduction

ABoston Terrier named "Bill" was the inspiration for the "Lost Souls: Found!" series by Happy Tails Books™. In 2008 two-year-old Bill was released from the small puppy mill cage where he'd spent his life, and put out to auction. When MidAmerica Boston Terrier Rescue took him into their care, he was in horrible shape. Overweight and terrified, he simply cowered in the back of his crate.

He was adopted out, but then quickly returned due to his poor psychological state. The family wanted a dog to play ball with, but all Bill could do was shiver and shake. It may seem callous, but they knew they hadn't the patience or desire to embark on the long road to rehab, and ultimately did the right thing by returning him to the rescue group.

As if things weren't bad enough for Bill, tragedy struck again when he and another female Boston broke free from their foster home's yard. The female, a socialite, was recovered within minutes. Bill, on the other hand, confused and afraid, went into hiding. He hid so well that he eluded an intensive community search brigade and somehow survived for three weeks, alone in a woodlands area where coyotes have dens. When he was finally spotted by a jogger, he weighed thirteen pounds (down from twenty-three), and was only a quarter mile from where he first escaped! Captured and delivered to

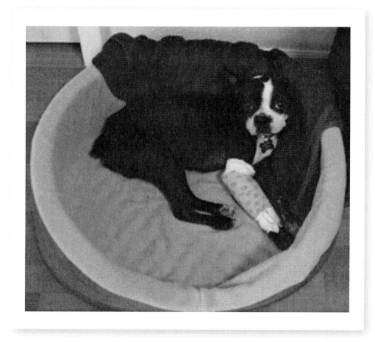

a shelter, he was so hurt, sickly and scared that the shelter didn't even know if they could save him.

Fortunately, Bill's microchip reunited him with his foster family. The shelter and the family jointly decided he deserved a chance. And so, Bill began the long road to rehab with deadness in his eyes. He barely moved or even looked around. A deep gash on his front leg required bi-weekly visits to the vet for bandage changes and laser treatments to help stimulate healing, but this physical injury was nothing compared to the tremendous psychological trauma poor Bill had been exposed to his entire life. He was so scared that for the first few months back in foster care he had to be carried outside to potty. As the pattern continued, it seemed Bill would never find happiness; but then, after four months, a glimmer of hope appeared...

With the help of other dogs at the dog park and a fantastic trainer, Bill began to come around. He transitioned from waiting to leave at the dog park gate, to becoming the star quarterback (kind of like that movie "Rudy," he's small but fierce!). With positive reinforcement training, daily "drags" turned into races and potty time became an exciting reason to dance around in circles.

These days, the first thing people notice about Bill is how his right hind leg flies out sideways as he sprints to greet them with a big smile on his face. This has nothing to do with his injuries, he's just trying to run and wag his stubby little corkscrew tail at the same time. Bill's always trying to do two things at once to make up for his lost "puppyhood," like bark and yawn at the same time when the car arrives at his favorite trailheads! He runs up rocks like a mountain goat and rolls down hills like a ninja, all the while making sure that his mommy is close by to share in the fun.

The light in this world burns brighter now that it has returned to Bill's eyes. This gentle, loving, lost soul has been found and has since touched the hearts of everyone who meets him.

Kyla Duffy, Bill's Foster (and Now Forever) Mom

Inspirational Stories of Adopted Boston Terriers

D o Bostons have tea parties? Are all rescued dogs a handful? How does fostering work? Is there such a thing as a dog that can't climb stairs? The stories on the following pages will answer these questions and more!

Mommy Can't Come to the Phone Now!

Dylan is a handsome boy! He is a deep red and bright white Boston Terrier; a bit on the BIG side, weighing 33lbs with a tail bent like a lightning bolt to give him superhero speed. He has a tongue that should fit in a hippopotamus's mouth and the softest feet I have ever felt. His favorite toy is a "pink" tennis ball (real men have pink tennis balls), but he also likes to rip the appendages off his Boston sister Morgan's favorite "kitties." Dylan is quite the character and we love him.

Like so many other unfortunate dogs, Dylan's life started at a puppy mill where he called a 2'x2', poop-filled cage his home. For whatever reason, he was put out to auction at the age of two and found himself in foster care in Nebraska with MidAmerica Boston Terrier Rescue. Skinny from not being fed regularly and with toes that were spread out from standing on the wire, Dylan was a sight for sore eyes.

Because he knew nothing of the outside world, Dylan was far from pleased about his release. Things that other dogs take for granted simply terrified him. In short order, he was bathed and his nails were trimmed—his first time receiving a spa treatment—then he was neutered, vaccinated and micro chipped at the vet. To him, this new situation seemed much, much worse than the previous one.

Life at his foster family's house was filled with foreign experiences. For the first time, he mingled freely with people. He walked on a variety of flooring surfaces like carpet, hardwood, tile and grass that were all so different from his cage. He didn't know what to do with doorways and had no concept of pottying outside.

A month after arriving in foster care, Dylan was sent from Nebraska to what was to be his "forever home" in Colorado. However, he was still far from being comfortable in the role of a family pet, and the new family was equally as far from being comfortable with him. They changed their minds quickly and gave Dylan back to rescue.

As a foster mom and volunteer coordinator for the rescue group, I picked up Dylan and brought him to my house. He was greeted by my spunky Boston "Morgan" and my ailing German Shepherd "Zane," both of whom scared the vomit out of him, literally. He found solace in the kennel I had set up in the corner of my living room, and for a few days came out as little as possible. He wanted nothing to do with Morgan and me, but quickly he warmed up to Zane and followed him everywhere.

Having a strong German Shepherd to look up to must have given him great confidence. On our walks, Dylan would lean up against Zane the entire way around the block, but Zane didn't mind at all. He was old and succumbing to cancer, but still let the poor Boston believe that he was a strong ally in his new world. Tragically, two weeks after Dylan came into foster care at my house, Zane passed away. Morgan, Dylan and I were all left feeling quite lost. We no longer had our protector. I couldn't stop crying, Morgan hid behind the sofa, and the little progress Dylan had made went back to square one.

About a week after Zane's death, I came out from under the dark cloud and allowed the sun to shine on my life once again. I decided that Morgan and I needed Dylan as much as he needed us, so before I could turn back, I quickly called the rescue group and told them that I was keeping Dylan. I could hardly explain the decision to myself, let alone anyone who asked "why" I was adopting this oversized, emotional mess of a dog.

At this point, I still hadn't even petted Dylan. I would grab his harness as he ran by me so I could pet his head and feed him chicken. As I felt his tense muscles relax, I would let him go and say "GOOD BOY!" This process gradually turned into a strong bond between Dylan and me, and he became "my dog." Now he followed ME everywhere and leaned against

ME as we walked around the block. I had become Dylan's great "Zane!"

Dylan grew so attached to me that when he would see my car pull up from work each day, he went completely CRAZY! He would bark madly and run all over the house. When I walked through the door, he was so overwhelmed with excitement that he would jump up and bite me, usually leaving bruises and puncture marks all over my arms and stomach. I had worked so many months on creating this bond that I couldn't yell or discipline him over the excitement he had for my happy homecoming. So... I got inventive. I strategically placed a bucket of toys outside the front door. As I walked in the house, I would shove a toy in Dylan's mouth so that he couldn't bite me. This worked well; no bruises for me and Dylan would run through the house with his toy, equally as excited as he was when he used to have "me" in his mouth!

To my surprise, after a month of this Dylan began frantically searching for his own toy when he saw my car pull into the driveway. One day I entered the house expecting to find my overly excited Boston with a toy in his mouth, but instead he found the one he thought was my personal favorite—the cordless telephone! He ran through the house growling and barking, all the while slobbering into the buttons of the phone. Again, instead of scolding him, I considered this "making progress!"

Dylan was improving in all aspects of his recovery, and Morgan was accepting her new, not so much of a German Shepherd, little brother. She started coming out from behind the sofa and wanting to teach Dylan how to play. They were a bit awkward at first. For example, every time Morgan would play tug of war with Dylan, he would panic and try to EAT the toy. It would usually end with his choking on a rope toy and my saving the day by pulling it out of his esophagus.

After months of choking, Dylan and Morgan are now "playtime professionals." They run through the house chasing one another like 800 lb. gorillas. Just like brother and sister, they love to be with each other, and still get on one another's nerves. They fight over toys and keep each other company when I am at work.

Dylan's road to recovery from puppy mill life has been long, and we still have obstacles to overcome. To Morgan and me, it's worth all the time, medical expenses and accidents on the floor. Dylan wasn't the perfect fit for any family, but he is the perfect fit for ours. We love every last oversized, awkward pound of him.

Jami David

Life Starts as Twelve

One December night I received an urgent call asking me to pick up an elderly, female Boston Terrier who'd recently been dropped off at the county animal shelter and was not doing well. She possibly had mange, and needed to be rescued quickly. Seeing as the shelter was about an hour away and scheduled to close in an hour, my husband and I made the quick decision to go and get her. We expected the coordinator from the rescue group who initially contacted us to call back with instructions on where to take this dog, but instead she asked if we could possibly keep her as a foster. It turned out that all the other foster parents were full! We had just adopted our own puppy mill rescue a few weeks prior, but this old gal sounded like she was in need of desperate care and we couldn't abandon her.

When I saw her at the shelter, I couldn't keep back my tears. A mangy Boston Terrier stood before me in a worn sweater, shaking and in terrible shape. Her eyes were sad and she was missing most of her hair. The paperwork that the owner filled out said, "Kristi, 12 years old, likes car rides." That was it.

At home we set her up in a large crate with lots of blankets that was away from the other dogs so she wouldn't be scared. I was afraid to take off the sweater, but knew it had to go. I carefully peeled it away and was absolutely horrified at what I saw. She was covered in puss-filled sores, almost completely bald from her neck back and had scratched herself raw. She was actively oozing from her head to her tail, and the sweater had been on her for so long that it was almost impossible to remove completely.

She was so dear and so passive. She let us examine her without a sound. She literally looked relieved and thankful. I stared at her little face, and I said to her, "Mom Mom, you are home now, and we are going to make sure that you get better. We will take care of you." This dog was clearly in need of a major change, and "Mom Mom" seemed so appropriate that it became her name from that point on.

We took Mom Mom to the vet two days later and had her evaluated. She had the following medical problems: ulcers in both eyes; severe gingivitis with advanced tooth decay; an infected growth in her mouth; yeast infections in both ears; atopic dermatitis on her skin with possible mange; open wounds on her back and hind quarters; arthritis; a heart murmur and 28 allergies (we found this out after extensive allergy testing).

We treated her for all of her major health issues, and then began taking her to The Animal Wellness Center Holistic Vet in PA. Mom Mom began her recovery and has continued her treatment without complaint. She recovered from most of her ailments. A year later we are still treating her for her allergies with shots every two weeks and a special diet with supplements. Mom Mom has grown most of her hair back, and the sores and ulcers are long gone.

The irony is that Mom Mom was considered un-adoptable because of her age and medical issues, yet she has thrived with us. The shelter had an overabundance of younger, healthier dogs arriving daily that required them to make the tough decision to euthanize her. Thankfully they called our rescue group first, and instead, Mom Mom is now considered a permanent foster dog and has become the queen of our house. She loves meatloaf and peanut butter, and nothing makes her happier than a big pile of blankets.

While we wonder what her first 12 years of life were like, we choose instead to focus on the cliché that "everyone deserves a second chance," and this is hers!

Mom Mom was the first elderly dog that we ever took in. She is low maintenance and never asks for anything. She is housebroken and just loves to hang out and watch the activity in the house. She is kind and gentle, just like a Mom Mom! We can't possibly imagine our home without Mom Mom there watching over all of us.

Mom Mom is a living example that miracles do happen. She's proof that no matter how bad things get, if you open yourself up to love and compassion, it will eventually find you.

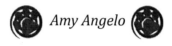 *Amy Angelo*

A Fine Gentleman

Part 1—The Relay Race

I'd wanted a dog for a long time, so on my quest I became an Internet "adoptable dog" search junkie. Combing the web each day was a daunting activity since I really didn't know what type of dog I wanted and they all looked cute, playful and friendly. However, one day I came across a listing for a Boston Terrier named "Fargo," and I knew I had found "the one."

The posting about Fargo said that this dog, who looked like a distinguished gentleman, had spent his entire life in a cage at a puppy mill. He was born into servitude and used as a breeding machine for someone's financial gain. I was horrified and deeply saddened by this.

Fargo's story inspired me to further research puppy mill dogs. I could not imagine how people could buy dogs from pet stores when so many needed to be rescued. The answer came to me at work when I told my colleagues about Fargo and they recommended I get a "normal" dog. Clearly they had not seen or read what I had. If by "normal" they meant one that came from a pet store, I didn't want anything to do with it. I had set my heart on helping to give a dog—which already had a very bad life—a very good life now.

More than ever, I was convinced that dog rescue was the way to go, and so I inquired about Fargo. A long discussion with his foster mom solidified what I already knew; Fargo was the one. With the decision made, the new challenge became getting him, since Fargo was being fostered near Omaha, NE and I was in Colorado Springs, CO.

After many emails and phone calls Fargo was booked on a road trip. The plan was for a multi-day relay race with Fargo as the torch. The final "runner" was a trucker who would deliver him to Limon, CO, where I was to finally meet my new little man. I asked myself, "What could go wrong?"

It never occurred to me that a tanker could explode in the road—which can, and did, happen. The event itself was merely a delay. The problem was I didn't have a cell phone and so couldn't let anyone know I was now stuck.

The police directed me to follow a trucker down an icy, muddy road. While that, too, seemed like a good plan, the mud splatter from his tires caused me to quickly lose sight of him. I now had no idea where I was and no way to contact the trucker, so I did what anyone would; I plowed ahead.

What could have been a disaster worked out in the end as I pulled into the truck stop just as the trucker carrying Fargo was filling his tank. It turns out that truckers have a way of "knowing things," and this one knew I was going to be late. In other words, he heard about the accident on his CB radio.

We went to a safe spot and Fargo and I greeted each other for the first time. Shaking and obviously terrified, my brave little gentleman stood up tall and walked to me with as much calm as he could muster after a long uncertain journey. He looked at me. I looked at him. And for both of us it was love at first sight.

Part 2—Ladies First

A second chance at life is an opportunity for a new name for many rescued dogs. It gives the dog and owner an opportunity to leave the dog's past behind and begin anew. My immediate thought when I saw Fargo's adoption picture was that the old soul in the photo was more of a "Winston" than a "Fargo." "Winston" seemed especially appropriate since he was "dressed in a tux," eight years old, mellow and a bit shy.

So, after eight years in a puppy mill knowing nothing more than the cold cage walls that surrounded him, "Fargo" came into the warmth of my home as "Harry Winston Churchill."

While I thought that I would quickly begin teaching Winston new things once we got back home, I came to realize that it was actually *he* who was teaching *me* patience. My first reality check was that Winston was afraid of me. Even after a week of my unrelenting attempts at affection, he still ran to his kennel to hide at every chance. Once he went outside to potty, he never wanted to come in (especially if I was inside the door), and it felt safe to him to eat at mealtimes only if I was sitting down. The biggest surprise, however, was Winston's difficulty with stairs. Our home is a split-level, with most nighttime activities upstairs and daytime activities downstairs. I saw that he was stuck in the middle level and found it as a metaphor for his current state of being. In his mind he must have been torn between the torment of the past and uncertainty of the future—a lost little soul stuck between fear and hope.

Days of unsuccessfully trying to persuade him with treats left me thinking that we might never surmount the stairs. It was at the point of despair that I realized I needed to be creative. I leashed him and got on my tummy to show him how it is done. Slowly, step by step, I crawled, tugged and encouraged. I thought I might have failed again but slowly, so slowly, one timid paw after another went down and we were braving the big scary stairs! Before we knew it, we were both at the bottom—a surprised and unscathed Winston and me looking only slightly worse for the wear.

Since then, Winston has become every bit the gentleman I saw in his adoption picture and I am proud to be his lady. I wouldn't quite call him a "normal" dog but I don't mind. Participating in his incremental progress and celebrating small things, like learning to go down the stairs, leaves a big impact on my heart. We still have a long way to go but Winston and I will walk (or crawl) this path together, paw by paw, to a place where he can live out the rest of his days feeling safe, relaxed and loved.

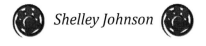 *Shelley Johnson*

A "Snort" Break

The Granddogs: Our poodle had passed on, our daughter had grown, and we were thriving as "empty nesters." We shamelessly fawned over dogs in the neighborhood, and fantasized about taking them home (if only for a day or two). When our daughter began fostering Boston Terriers we inadvertently fell into the perfect situation: we instantly became foster grandparents! We play with them and love them as we would with grandchildren, and when our time is through, they go back to their home. The only difference is that they don't yet have a permanent home and occasionally have special needs. For us, the troubled dogs have been even more fun as we get to see incremental progress each time we catch up with them. Maybe for a "regular" dog getting out of a safe spot to get a drink of water is no big deal... for our dogs it is a chance to celebrate with a piece of cheese—humans and dogs alike. Yum! –*Carol and Dennis Duffy*

Zzzzz...: After a few "interesting" months with us, we decided to take Vinnie for some training. He loved learning and was very good at it, except for the fact that he would fall asleep in class! His usual bedtime was at 7pm, and the class would go on until 7:45. It never failed that 7pm sharp, no matter what the instructor was doing, it was "lights out" for Vinnie! –*Jackie McClain*

There's a Microscope in My Mouth, I Swear! When we adopted Chelsea we got more than just a dog... it turns out she is also an entomologist! She loves to sit outside with us and study the bugs in our yard. She likes many bugs, but Cicadas are her favorite. She gallops around while "studying" them with her tongue and teeth. When she walks up to us and her jaw is buzzing, we know it's a cicada! –*June Duncan*

Enabled

Found as a stray, Tinker ended up in a high-kill shelter in the Metro Atlanta area. Luckily someone there had the sense to call The Small Dog Rescue (a no-kill shelter), which took her in. They cleaned up an ulcer on her eye and a tumor on her leg, and then crossed their fingers that her new family would materialize. They waited and waited but received no applications for a year. It looked like Tink was going to become a "forever foster."

At the time, I was finishing up my music therapy internship and exploring the idea of adding a dog to our family. I've always been head over heels for Bostons, as I grew up with one who was feisty, bold and a whole lot of love wrapped into a small package. Being fiercely loyal myself, other breeds just didn't have a chance! We looked and looked until, on Christmas Eve, there, on page 15 of the Boston Terriers on Petfinder.com (yes, there were that many needing homes), we finally found her!

She was old and blind—she had been in a fight while at the shelter and lost vision in her one good eye—but she spoke to my heart. Having worked with children and adults with special needs as a music therapist, the idea of bringing a dog with a disability into our home made perfect sense. Her profile stated that, despite her past, she knew how to love and trust. Upon reading her biography I was positive that she would fit perfectly into our house and family.

I looked at my husband and with the saddest face I could muster asked, "Can we adopt her?"

My puppy dog eyes apparently worked, because in the next moment I was emailing the shelter asking if we could apply. Their policy excluded people in our area from adopting (we were too far away from their headquarters), but I thought I would try anyway.

I'm glad I wrote because we received an email on Christmas morning saying that we could apply for her! "It really IS Christmas!" I shouted as I ran down the stairs.

Being approved to apply turned out to be a double-edged sword kind of gift. Apparently two other families applied at the same time we did, so our joy quickly turned to fear and apprehension. We exchanged emails, phone calls and applications with the shelter for over a month. We walked on eggshells thinking we would lose Tinker, but after a long, difficult wait, Tink's foster mom chose us! Upon hearing the news, my husband and I rented a car, packed a cooler full of food (we were rather broke, living on one income at the time), and made 12 hours worth of memories as we traveled to Atlanta to pick this little one up.

We made plans with Tink's foster mom to meet at a Petco® store. I remember that waiting for them to arrive with Tink seemed like an eternity. Her foster was worried that we wouldn't like her; we were nervous that they wouldn't like us. What compounded our anxiety was that when we called to check in, someone from the rescue group told us that Tinker was going on a trip and wouldn't be at Petco®. We hoped that they were confused and that the trip she was taking was with us!

Sure enough, the long wait and uncertainty ended when her foster mom carried her in with tears in her eyes and we met our little heart dog, Tinker, for the first time. We signed forms, talked and shared. Her foster mom provided a bed and some clothing since Tinker was going to be a "northerner" now. We parted with teary eyes and thankful hearts.

Tinker came to us as an older dog but showed us that she could still learn and grow. We taught her to beg, and when she started jumping on company, we untaught her! She eventually learned that thunder wouldn't hurt her, and she began sleeping through the night during storms.

From the beginning, this has been an amazing journey of new discoveries every day! And while she is aging now, with her good and not so good days, she is still the most amazing dog I have ever met or owned. Her blindness doesn't impede her, and she is not afraid to love with all she has. People do not realize this confident little lady can't see a thing as she proudly walks down the street. Tinker is my heart and I am proud to be her seeing-eye person.

 *Nick and Vicki Rowe*

The Perfect Puppy

I took on the quest of finding a dog as I would any new subject...research, tenacity, and every detail laid out to perfection.

First I researched breeds, and discovered that the Boston Terrier fit my parameters. But not just any Boston. Not only did it have to have an excellent disposition and even temperament, but I was really particular about the markings being just right...Not too much white and not too much black on the face, with both front legs and paws being completely white. I became almost obsessed with finding a puppy that looked and behaved just the way I thought he/she should.

I'd learned a lot about the breed through library books, dog magazines, talking with breeders, visiting breeders, and through asking tons of questions, and had visions of making the perfect "potty-training" schedule. I had not really been around dogs since my childhood days on my parents' farm, so as a first-time adult owner, I prided myself in being completely prepared! The best dog for me was clearly a puppy from a reputable, local breeder so I could start out "fresh" with housetraining, obedience training, building trust and love from the ground up. I'd seen some rescue dogs online, but knew I couldn't properly care for one, as most seemed to have been through much trauma and neglect.

Naturally, as a Middle School Counselor, I wanted to wait for the perfect time when school was out in June to bring home my new "baby." I had a couple of reputable breeders selected, and was excited to make plans to meet the mothers and fathers of the litters arriving soon during the summer months.

However, as is often the case, the best laid plans go awry, and those sad faces I saw online at the rescue websites kept calling me back again. I could not get them out of my mind. And then one night I made the most unlikely decision: I found myself applying for one little dog simply described as "Lily: Five-year-old; released from breeder; mellow; sweet; and shares your pillow at night."

I completed the online adoption application, feeling nervous at the thought of caring for an older "rescue" dog – my preparation had been for the homecoming of my perfect puppy! I thought I'd just see what happened. After all, I had not really committed to anything, yet, had I?

Sure I had! After filling out the application there was no turning back. Lily's markings were beautiful and she had a face I couldn't resist. I received her on a Saturday morning the day before Easter and four days before my 39th birthday. She was my "Easter Lily!"

The first few weeks were not easy; and to be honest, I found them a bit frightening – I still wasn't confident that I could properly care for her. She was timid and weak, with low hanging nipples from her history as a puppy mill breeder. Our first night together was especially difficult for Lily; it rained and stormed, and she was extremely afraid of the thunder.

The weather pattern continued on and off for a few weeks so I took extra special care of her, which turned out to be an amazing bonding experience. Because of the time I spent comforting her, I was able to help her to relax more around loud noises. This, and practicing walking on a leash, has helped to build her confidence.

After our first few days together, Lily began to come out of her shell and I learned much about her. She turned out to be a loving little girl with a tremendous curiosity. From her reactions to things, I wondered if she ever saw the outside of her cage during her life at the puppy mill. Cars were new to her, as were people. She became playful when I came home to greet her from work, enjoyed our adventurous walks together, and knew when it was time to relax. These days, she still likes some alone time, is capable of entertaining herself, but loves to cuddle together in the evenings.

At the same time as I was finding out about Lily, I was pleased to discover that I, myself, was completely capable of taking care of her. When Lily seemed sad, I held her to reassure her and comfort her. And with patience and love Lily was improving on our walks. We made so much progress, in fact, that now we can jog together on full stretches of grassy areas around the lake, which makes her seem happy and energetic, and can only be good for me too!

I don't believe a brand new puppy would have had the impact on my life that Lily has. She's taught me love and compassion, and that everyone deserves a second chance. Her love for me is unconditional, and I believe I am more patient, understanding, and giving to others from Lily's example. Her trust increases daily, and she has shown me how to better trust others, as well. All in all, I believe Lily and I have rescued each other. I could not imagine my life without her now.

My perfect puppy turned out to be a perfect ex-puppy mill breeder.

 *April Thompson*

Peanuts

Our family had many Boxers when I was a child so I'm no stranger to dogs. When I got married my husband and I began showing them, and then decided to add a Boston Terrier to our family because the breed seemed like "mini-Boxers" to us. Tragically, one of our female Boxers named Bailey didn't see it that way. She randomly attacked Dior, the Boston we brought home, several months after his arrival. The innocent, little dog recovered from life-threatening wounds, but was always terrified of our house and of us so we thought it best to re-home him.

Since then, we've heard that Dior went on to become a successful show dog with his new family. As for Bailey, we realized that she was, in fact, volatile and dangerous. We had to make the heartbreaking decision to euthanize her for the safety of others. We cried and agonized over it but knew it was the right thing to do.

After such a traumatic event, it was difficult for us to consider the addition of another dog to our family. Our son, however, became the driving force behind the idea of getting another Boston. He always loved dogs and especially missed Dior even though he only lived with us for a short time. For months he pestered us about getting another, and one day we finally gave in.

We thought we would give adoption a try even though we had always worked with private breeders in the past, so we found a local rescue group. We saw a large male named "Bos" on their website, and thought he would be a good fit to play with our Boxers. The only catch was that Bos didn't like men. Regardless, there was something special about him, so we wanted to give him a chance. The rescue group arranged transportation for Bos, and after months of waiting our son finally got his Boston Terrier.

We had many "what were we thinking?" moments following Bos' adoption, as we couldn't seem to show him that men were okay too. He didn't go near my son or husband, or even me for that matter. This was a strange experience for all of us since we were used to our fun-loving, confident Boxers. Bos just stayed in his crate as much as he could and barely came out to go potty.

After many disheartening months and almost giving up on him, I walked into the living room one day and saw Bos sitting on the floor by my husband's chair, looking completely content. His eyes were half shut and my husband was petting him!

I asked my husband what happened, and he replied "I made him love me one peanut at a time!" I had no idea that my husband had been secretly giving Bos peanuts—not that I wouldn't have approved—I just wouldn't have ever thought that peanuts could pave the way to our dog's heart!

These days, Bos plays happily with our Boxers, and when my husband is home, tends not to stray far from the side of his chair. He's now a momma's boy because I'm the one who feeds him, but so long as my husband continues with the peanuts, he'll have Bos as his sidekick. While he never turned out to be the perfect dog for our son he's our favorite "nut" and we love him.

 *Tamara Veal*

The Gracie Challenge

O ur Friday night was not your regular date night consisting of a movie and popcorn. Instead, I received a frantic call from the rescue group we work with saying that four dogs were going to be shot in the morning at a puppy mill in Sunbury, Pennsylvania. The Amish farmer was done breeding these dogs and had released them from their cages the day before, hoping that they would just run away. They did not. The dogs instead stayed on the property scavenging for food and water. It was still winter and freezing outside—where were they to go?

The members of the rescue group were panicked about how we were going to get the "death row" dogs into a safe home before it was too late. A compassionate friend managed to take the dogs from the farmer's property and bring them to her local vet where they were boarded overnight. My husband and I volunteered to make the two-hour drive in the rescue van to pick them up, regardless of the snow and rain. The thought of those dogs being out in that weather just killed us, and we wanted to get them into a home as soon as possible.

When we got to our destination we were horrified—the dogs didn't look like dogs at all! They were covered in mud, smelled like a sewer and barely had the energy to move. As I loaded them into the van, I looked through my tears into their tired eyes and attempted to reassure them that they would never be hurt again. I couldn't imagine how a human being could treat such beautiful creatures like trash, and just throw them away, like the farmer did. Even though they were covered in filth I wanted to hold them, love them and somehow take away their pain.

This was especially the case for the last dog we put in the van, a tiny female. Her body was emaciated with spine and ribs protruding. Her coat was dull and thin, and she was obviously starving. I knew from the second I saw her that there was no way she was ever going to leave my arms.

Since my husband and I picked up the dogs, we had the opportunity to choose which one we would foster. I pretended that there was a decision to make, but in my heart (and in his heart), we knew which dog was coming home with us—and we knew she would never leave.

We thought that a fitting name for the little one would be "Gracie," after the famous Brazilian Jiu Jitsu fighter Royce Gracie, who has had a long string of wins in a variety of fighting forums. He was known for issuing "The Gracie Challenge," an invitation to any fighter for a match without rules – no holds barred. Our poor little "Gracie" never issued that challenge, but appeared to be stuck in a lawless life anyway. Now she was in a fight for her life; and after all she had already survived, we were confident that she would win this time as well!

"Round one" was no easy victory for her. Like all our "new" mill moms, Gracie immediately went into heat at our home. It was a very difficult three months for us all—she bled heavily, and we could only console her with a heating pad and doggie diapers. Of course we got through it and then had her spayed, but our hearts were heavy for Gracie...as if she didn't have enough to deal with!

"Round two" was Gracie's mangled elbow that caused her to carry her leg like a purse when she walked. The vet deemed it impossible to fix because it had happened too long ago, and wasn't properly cared for at the time. He surmised she was probably stepped on by a large person or animal. At least she didn't appear to be in any pain. To this day she still holds up her front leg when she walks. My husband says she's "just styling" with her "purse." We think Gracie believes that too, because instead of letting it hold her back she prances around like debutant at a society ball!

The toughest battle that would last many rounds was dealing with Gracie's history of starvation. Not having much food available to her at the mill, she would gorge herself on dog food and then go looking for anything else she could eat in our home. Sucking food down like a vacuum cleaner, she'd then gag and throw up everything. This went on for a while without dire consequences until one day, when Gracie was eating her breakfast, she began to choke. She threw up, and her eyes grew very big and red before she fell over, unconscious!

Though we were alarmed, I tried to clear her mouth and throat of food as best I could while my husband performed CPR and rescue breathing on her. Time stood still. She was lifeless for what seemed like forever, even though it was probably only a minute or so. Then, suddenly, she opened her eyes and huffed! We both cried out with joy and relief... she was ok! After such an experience we were all exhausted. Gracie spent the rest of the day on the couch, and we spent it researching doggie CPR classes!

Gracie would have these choking episodes now and then without any warning. The vet said that there was no medical reason why they occurred, but that Gracie was probably just eating too fast (WAY TOO FAST!). We decided to hand feed her very slowly at every meal, which (knock on wood) seems to have solved the problem. Again, Gracie lived up to her name. She fought this match and won, just like Royce Gracie.

Gracie is now the troublemaker of our pack, and is ALWAYS getting into mischief. She is the smallest of the dogs, and will often sneak her way into situations the other dogs can't get into. She is a happy girl who loves to play non-stop, and she has long since forgotten her frightening days at the puppy mill. Royce Gracie may not yet be retired, but our "Gracie" has officially stepped out of the ring.

 *Amy Angelo*

A "Snort" Break

Back Seat Driver: "It has been a year now since Max took over as chief lap sitter and car companion. He takes a real dim view of my going off without him, but at least he now goes back in the house to wait for me. His original idea was to stay at the gate until I returned. He works diligently at scoping out my intentions. If I comb my hair or put on lipstick, he dashes out the door to be ready to get in the car." –Barbara Richards, 80 year old Boston Terrier Fan!

A Dog's Eye View

You'd think I'd be from Boston, being a Boston Terrier and all, but instead I'm a small town girl from Courtice, Ontario, Canada (my grandparents were immigrants!). I had to move from there after two years—it seems my human Mom couldn't handle my sister Tinker and me, two Boston *Terrors*. Ahem... I mean *Terriers*. We went to the shelter together, and luckily when my new Mom came to visit she picked me to take home! Yeah! No more being chased by a three-year-old kid with a vacuum; no more of my bratty sister, body slamming me and stealing my Kong®.

What's that? You want to know how I became the ray of sunshine in my new parents' lives that I am today? Get ready to read because I'm gonna tell you...

Day 1:

I arrived at my new digs in Waterloo, Ontario, and noticed there wasn't any food around. Oh no... Where in the "H. E. double hockey sticks" is my feed-yourself dog food dispenser? Not available around the clock? It's 5:00p.m. and NOW she comes out with the food? I should say so! She better get the snacks out later or someone will get a wet shoe! That's all I have to say.

OK, so now here we are, Day One, and where am I supposed to go potty? Out there? The snow is deeper than the Grand Canyon, for gosh sake! Get the shovel going lady!

I'm four hours into it when I notice another thing missing! My bed! Where the heck am I supposed to sleep? I checked out the rest of the house and it seemed ok. Not a palace but it will do. It's kinda quiet though...no stinker Tinker, no kid... Guess that's ok when I'm napping; I'll make some noise later! There had better be a sunny spot for me. I'm not licking these people until I get some answers.

It's bedtime now and I still can't find my bed! I guess I'll follow Mom and that guy who is always here upstairs to see what kind of accommodations they have. It better be good! Huh...they're patting their king-sized bed like I'm supposed to sleep between them on a big comfy, down-filled blanket. Treats! Treats in bed! OMG! "Good night, Nicki" is right! Guess I could give her one small kiss. Not him though.

Day 2:

Mom's gone to work. That guy is outside doing something—all I know is that he's not paying attention to me. Doesn't he know I have needs! Hellllloooooo! Maybe he needs a wakeup call. When the door opens, I'm going to run like the wind. Here I go!

This is me doing Mach 1 up the street and around a couple of corners. Oh, oh. Where am I? What was I thinking? It's freakin' cold out here in a huge snowstorm; maybe that wasn't such a good idea after all.

So I'm walking down the road and a car stops. A lady gets out, looks at me and calling something—who knows what she was saying. Crazy gal, what was SHE doing out here in this weather? Nothing to do with me... She hopped back in her car and drove right up beside me and showed me some old Cherrios®. Now food's always good, but as I checked it out, she put a bear hug on me and put me in the car. Turns out it was my Mom!

Apparently that guy called my mom at work in a panic and told her I bolted out the door, and she was NOT happy with him (I'm flawless!).

Never again... Now when I get to go free I stick to her like glue. It took about a month before I'd even go down the front steps of our house on my own; I don't want to lose these guys—it's warm in their house!

It's funny, that guy didn't pay attention to me but I actually felt kind of bad for getting him in trouble. I figured I'd better lay low and behave for a bit. Just a bit.

Later...

Wait, are those some toys, a new leash and a bully stick on the floor? Could it be for me!? Joy! What was I thinking? I am SO important!

My friend told me not to ask what a bully stick is – just eat it. So I did. As Rachel Ray says, YumO! She's my favorite. I love watching her and the Dog Whisperer®.

Now that the TV's off, it's crazy time! These people better not get in my path or I'll MOW them down! Oh, oh hardwood floors. That's gonna hurt. Luckily Dad softened my landing with a pillow at the right time. Did I say DAD!?! Huh. He's not so bad. I GUESS I'll try not to growl at him so much.

Long story short...new Mom and Dad spoil me rotten! I couldn't be happier if a giant Milk Bone® fell from the sky. Thanks, Mom and Dad, I owe you a lick!

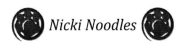 *Nicki Noodles*

(Translated by "Mom" Darlene Nevery)

Foster Failure

As near as we can tell Ruby was born in the mid 1990's in a puppy mill. The mill was in the hills of Kentucky and was typical of all mills; essentially it was nothing more than a large cold, pole barn, built for one purpose—to make money.

Ruby was a perfect puppy mill dog—beautifully marked and good at breeding. For eight years she was bred, void of love and human contact, except for feeding and breeding time when she was tossed in with another dog to make some more money for the miller. Her existence could only be described as lonely, scary and painful. Both health care and kindness were equally neglected.

After years and years of breeding, Ruby's reward was more of the same neglect. With rotten teeth and heartworm she was dumped at a local shelter. Nameless at the time, and even more afraid, Ruby found herself in another cold cage with a still uncertain future.

Midwest Boston Terrier Rescue turned out to be the miracle that she needed. Despite the fact that she was fairly old and very ill, they enthusiastically took her in. Out of kindness, they spent more money on Ruby to make her well than they would ever recover from adoption fees and donations, but they didn't care. To them, rescue can be expensive but saving a life is priceless.

Next *our* miracle occurred. As fosters affiliated with Midwest Boston Terrier Rescue, we received the request to foster Ruby. Of course, we said "yes," and Ruby came into our lives with more moxie than anyone I have ever known. For someone who only weighed 18 pounds, she took up more space than a 150-pound Great Dane. Her presence seemed huge because wherever we went she was right there with us, her smiling face ready for whatever fun thing was coming next.

Because of Ruby's amazing personality, it only took us a week to decide to adopt her. In rescue we call that a *foster failure*. It happens to us all. We say we are fostering, and then one of our pups wiggles its way into our hearts and never leaves. So it was with Ruby.

We believe that the day Ruby came into foster care is truly when her life began. At the age of eight she was like a naughty puppy. She scaled our 6' fence like a cat, left dead moles on our pillows and danced around our heads until we would wake up and notice, and <u>always</u> sat on my husband's school papers when he was trying to finish grading them.

The one habit we could not break was her jumping on the kitchen table. She had clearly never seen one before she came into our home and thought it was a good place to stand. We inadvertently reinforced her opinion of it by paying immediate attention to her for doing it. We would gently remove her, but she loved the attention so would just leap up again. Life was like a party to our Ruby; a big huge party that never ended. Grass, pillows, people, love (and tables!)... to her it may as well have been her birthday every day.

Late one winter Ruby started to have seizures from a brain tumor. After two weeks of medical issues, her human children who babysit her, "the Bunce-kids," came to visit her on a Thursday night. She was very sick and was having difficult time breathing. For one last time our Ruby made them smile... With all of the effort she had, she once again landed in the middle of the kitchen table so she could be close to them. It had been quite some time since she had mustered the energy.

We held her all night as her breathing slowed and her heart tired. The next morning her wonderful doctor, Don Hitzemann helped her cross the "Rainbow Bridge," as we gently whispered our good-byes.

Like all puppy mill girls, Ruby never took anything for granted. The pain of losing her was immense but we took heart in the fact that she successfully fit 14 years of life into the five that remained. She always played like it was the best game ever, walked as if she were on air, and loved us more than anyone deserved to be loved.

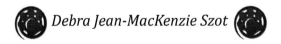 *Debra Jean-MacKenzie Szot*

Youth Revisited

I've just received my first invitation to join AARP. My bones creak in the morning, and ache in the evening. A big night on the town is now dinner out and home by 9:30pm. I'm at peace with being old and sedentary.

In my adult life, I have been owned by three Boston Terriers and one Border Collie. Kaitlin, my beautiful Border Collie, lived 16 long years and other than annual vet visits, she had but one abscessed tooth. She died as she lived—low maintenance and peacefully. Kip was my 19-year-old Boston who, although deaf and blind, may have lived on for a while longer had I not thought that he deserved his dignity, and crossed him over while he still had some. Then there was Kelsey, the 15-year-old Boston who had enough accidents and issues for an entire novel throughout her many years. She died after two final years, dealing with deafness, arthritis and a mass in her liver. Holden was my first Boston rescue, joining me at what we estimated to be age five. During the next five years that he was with me, we battled cancer, old injuries, food bowl fears and finally a brain tumor.

Sadly, Kelsey and Holden left me within eight weeks of each other in the summer of 2008. I was suddenly dog-less for the first time in 20 years. I was heartbroken, financially broken and lost, but also feeling the tiniest bit liberated. I had spent the last six months carrying dogs up and down the stairs, on and off the furniture, buying and hand feeding rotisserie chickens and baby food hot dogs. I washed bedding for me and the dogs daily, and carpeted my hardwoods in piddle pads. I turned down social invitations, and steadfastly refused to travel. I was on a first name basis with two local vets, and even had their cell phone numbers.

I assumed I would adopt an older dog after a time, probably a rescue that would come to me as a foster and just stay. Then, about four weeks after Holden passed, my friend, at least that's what she claims to be, sent me an e-mail with a tiny matchbook size head shot of a Boston who was currently at our local Animal Control office.

"Thanks," I replied sarcastically.

As I've transported several Boston rescue babies, I'm intimately familiar with the pound and its phone number.

"Hello," I said into the telephone receiver. I listened as the coordinator explained that it was a boy, and that he had been picked up by animal control, but no one had claimed him. "He's sick with an upper respiratory infection," she said. "There is quarantine at the SPCA (where this dog would go to be put up for public adoption) and I don't know if he will make it up there or not."

I was immediately alarmed about the possibility of "not," which would mean the worst for this dog.

"I'll adopt him," I said.

"Thanks so much. We'll have him checked over by our vet and call you when he is ready," she said.

She called three days later to let me know I could pick him up that afternoon. In that conversation, I finally got around to asking his age.

"Eight weeks."

Well, the tremor some of you may have felt across the country in the fall of 2008 was me shrieking, "8 WEEKS!!!"

And, that is how the old lady with the old dogs re-entered the world of puppies. I spend my time now chasing him, removing things from his mouth, walking him two miles a day on my arthritic feet just to wear him out, taking him to doggy day care and dragging him to obedience classes. I have spent more time shimming under my bed then I would have ever thought possible.

His name is Riley the Roo, he is fiercely independent and head strong. He challenges me daily as I remind myself that I am supposed to be smarter than he is.

I blew gently into his face the third day I had him and he responded by putting his paw over my mouth, forever sealing our bond. I have traded prescription meds, eye droppers and acupuncture treatments for Nylabones®, training collars, and chew toys. I am exhausted, frustrated and absolutely thrilled. He is my delight and joy, and I'm in better shape than I have been in years!

 *Peggy Longenecker*

A "Snort" Break

A "Jack" of All Trades Named Seamus: When we adopted Seamus, he had just had his eyelashes frozen because they were growing towards his eyes. At first, we thought he looked a little bit like a "Jack-O-lantern!" However, we quickly discovered that he had an adventurous streak in him that reminded us more of "Jack Sparrow" (Pirates of the Caribbean®) . . . in more ways than one. Not only did he like to explore, it turned out that he liked to loot as well! And not just any old booty. Our little Seamus was a "panty" pirate! We caught him hoarding bra parts and panties in the yard! We eventually broke him of the habit, but he'll never live down his reputation. –*Audrey Crawford*

Yee-Haw! I've always loved horses but never thought I would be so lucky to adopt a dog who loved them too. Some dogs are lap dogs, but it turns out my Odie is a saddle dog. He is so content riding my horse that he falls asleep on the horse's back! –*Crystal Lindsey*

The Supermodel: Mickey spent the first three years of his life living outside in a cage. He had signs of frostbite and an eye puncture wound, causing him partial blindness. Regardless, he knows he's beautiful! He loves to have his picture taken which is convenient for me since I'm a photographer. In the "nude" or in Armani®, it doesn't matter to him. He's a ham! –*Morgan Miller (Editor's Note: See Mickey on the front cover!)*

What'd You Call Me?

There once was a small, shy and very scared Boston Terrier named....well, at that time she had no name. She came from a puppy mill that bred her time and time again. She was obese, filthy and her feet were funny looking. She needed medical care, so off she went to the vet. Her toes were splayed and swollen; her nipples hung low to the ground. When they spayed her, they found tons of tiny little bones in her uterus. Apparently, she had repeatedly miscarried, yet not completely. The miller didn't bother to clean her out after her failed deliveries and just let the pups' bones sit inside of her womb.

When she went into foster care, she got a bath and a name: Kayla. She took to it instantly and began to blossom. The road was long—between potty training, getting to know humans and other dogs and learning to do stairs—it took some time. What didn't take much time was for her to find a patient family who loved her.

You see, we had lost our dear Sammie (male Boston Terrier) to a terrible disease called IMHA (Immunity Mediated Hemolytic Anemia) the same month Kayla was rescued. We were devastated, as was Sabbie, our female Boston Terrier. Sabbie and Sammie grew up together and when Sammie died, Sabbie became very depressed and withdrawn. We knew that we had to get another dog, ready or not! We decided to adopt another Boston from a local rescue group, and were contacted a few days after putting in our application about a possible match.

Kayla's foster mom, Tammy, called us and told us Kayla's story. I fell in love with her without even seeing a picture! We enthusiastically agreed to adopt her, and arranged to meet the foster mom and Kayla.

As we had expected from our conversation with Tammy, Kayla was a bit shy when she first came to our home. She didn't know how to play with toys and couldn't get up the steps or onto the couch. She was very fearful of my husband and my son, and glued herself to my side. I could tell she'd been a puppy mill girl.

Kayla and Sabbie got along very well, and became fast friends. Kayla struggled with her potty training, but eventually learned to go outside. She still struggles with being around men but isn't as fearful as she was in the beginning.

After adopting Kayla we took in two other Boston Terriers. One was an elderly shelter rescue and the other a puppy mill mom. Kayla immediately took to the mill mom, somehow knowing that she was like her. She blossomed in her role as teacher, helping our new mill mom to play, run and jump. They even learned how to go up the steps together and have been inseparable since the very first day.

We've found that each foster dog that comes into our home gets taken under Kayla's wing. She soothes them, shows them the ropes and calms them down. She teaches them about life after the mill and will even sleep next to them to provide comfort.

Kayla is the comedian of the house; she waddles around and pounces here and there, chasing nothing at all. She loves scratching her back on the sidewalk and eating, although she is a bit on the heavy side. She hates being called fat, and prefers instead to think of herself as fluffy. If you call her "Fatty," she will stare you down until you take it back!

In her new life Kayla thrives with an abundance of human love and doggie friendship. The terrified terrier is now both teacher and class clown. It may have taken some time for her to figure out life in a home, but it took no time at all for us to learn that because of her, our home is now complete.

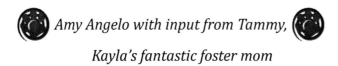

Amy Angelo with input from Tammy,
Kayla's fantastic foster mom

Eyes Only for You

I didn't grow up with dogs, and never really wanted one until my kids started getting older and more independent. I realized that my growing unease was the all-too-common "empty nest" feeling parents experience as their kids become adults. I decided a dog might be just the thing to create some new noise in our home. My plan was to begin researching breeds so that in six years when my youngest graduated I would maybe have found the right dog and be ready to adopt (yes, I'm a planner)...

Although I thought a dog would be a long ways off for us, I kept an eye on petfinder.com regularly to see what dogs were available for adoption. After only a few weeks, I narrowed my search down to a few different breeds. I decided to go with a Boston Terrier, not only because of all their wonderful qualities, but also because it was the breed that my now-deceased mother had when she was a little girl. I was looking for a dog with a medium build that loved walks and car rides and people in general. There was only one hitch—I couldn't stand the big, protruding eyes! They just freaked me out.

After weeks of looking through Boston Terrier profiles online, I came across a story of a 3-year-old named Odie who was surrendered because his family had had a baby. His side view portrait showed a cute, shmooshed face and stocky build, and from what I could see in the pictures, his eyes didn't seem to protrude. Though my youngest was still in school, I couldn't help but change my plan and apply for this dog. He looked like he had so much spunk and would be fun to have around!

I went to his foster parent's home to meet him and there, from the top of the stairs, he stood smiling at me... with eyes that looked like they were about to fall out of his head! They were so "googly" that I couldn't even tell which way he was looking! My heart sank, but before I knew it, he was in my arms, washing my face with slobbery doggie love.

After such an outpouring I was helpless but to "look the other way" about his eyes and take him home. Today Odie's eyes are my favorite part of him. I think they are beautiful. They talk to me! I even made a song up about them to the tune of "Sweet Caroline" by Neil Diamond. It goes "Sweet Odie

Pie, you're the cutest little guy, you have the most beautiful eyes, sweet Odie pie." Something like that...

I really lucked out on such a great dog with amazing character and expressive eyes. These days I wonder whether he thought *I* was the one with the weird-looking eyes when I first met him. If so, I'm glad he was able to overlook it because I couldn't "see" a future without him!

 *Kirsten Lahr*

Looking Glass Self

My grandparents had Boston Terriers throughout my childhood and I loved them, so when it came time for me to get a dog it was an easy choice. When I want something, I am focused until I complete my task, and at that time the task was to find a Boston Terrier. My search took me to the Northeast Boston Terrier Rescue's website where I submitted an application. I should have foreseen what was coming when I was immediately approved. I now know that I was one of the most sought after types of applicants for all the pups who come with "issues," because I had no dogs, cats or kids, own my home and have a fenced yard.

I quickly got a call about a dog named Scooter. After speaking at length with Scooter's foster mom, Robin, I knew that he was my dog. Honestly, I don't think I retained a word she said about his issues, all I remembered was his name, and that he was three years old, weighed 13 pounds and he could be mine. I kept thinking, "Who would give up this dog?"

It must have been fate because the adoption was scheduled on my birthday (let's just say it was my 29th... again). My mom and I drove two and half hours to meet my furry soul mate with a truckload of new dog supplies waiting at home. When we saw a car pull up at the meeting place with Bostons bouncing around in the window, I knew this was it!

Two beautiful Bostons jumped out, and I was ecstatic at the thought that one of them was him. However, it took only a second for me to notice the third dog and my heart sank. He was partially bald on his head and legs, with an odd wavy tail and spindly little legs, not at all what I pictured! The shock must have shown because I remember my mom whispering, "He's cute, I know you will fall in love with him!" She quickly scooped him up so Robin and I could complete the paperwork and I could take this all in.

I decided on "Wilbur" for Scooter's new name, because he looked and snorted like the pig in "Charlotte's Web." Within a day I was completely in love with him and able to overlook his "unique" appearance. However, as he became more comfortable and his true personality emerged, I found that my beloved "Wilbs" was the most highly-strung dog imaginable! He would go into a blind frenzy when he saw a dog or a person, and even bit visitors who came to my home. He also exhibited separation anxiety by chewing his beds. My new task became the taming of the 13-pound wild beast I'd lost my heart to.

This is where my tenacity came in handy. If Wilbur thought he could win, then he didn't know who he was up against. I started endless Internet searches, read books and called every trainer in the phone book. I studied harder than I had at college! After being turned away by two trainers because of his aggression, and another trainer telling me that it is probably genetic and there wasn't any hope, we finally found one who also loved a challenge and agreed to work with him. Of course, this trainer was the most expensive, but I decided I had no choice.

Anyone who has dealt with serious issues in their pet will agree that it weighs on you 24/7, but after many months of very hard work I finally felt back in control. I was willing to change my life to keep Wilbs but I knew that wasn't fair to either one of us. I clung faithfully to the idea that through hard work, consistency and leadership we could have a "normal life," and finally that dream came to fruition.

Our journey together has turned us into quite a pair. Today, Wilbs is my little "Pumpkin Pie," or "Grumpy Munchkin," depending on his mood. He'll never be a dog that I can take to the pet store or introduce to strangers, but "normal" isn't my thing anyway. Instead, I have adopted a mini-Einstein who is impeccably trained, finally trusts me and makes me laugh all the time. We have our good days and bad days, and some days beds get destroyed. But, overall, nobody's perfect and we're miles ahead of where we started.

Looking back at Robin's adoption write-up, I must have had rose colored glasses on while reading it. It was dead on, but I didn't even notice the challenges she had listed. I firmly believe now that destiny brought Wilbur and me together to teach me that life is messy; and that you learn more about yourself through the cleanup. I needed to be knocked over the head with a crazy dog to learn that lesson.

I'll never forget the trainer telling me, "No wonder this dog is a nervous wreck, you are one of the most high-strung people I've worked with!" After the shock of his brutal honesty wore off, I realized that looking at Wilbur was like looking in the mirror, and that we both could use some "remaking." Wilbur is my "looking glass self," and helping him has equally helped me to become a better person.

 Jodi Groff

A "Snort" Break

Fragile to FANTASTIC! Used as a puppy mill breeder, Dagney was never handled kindly and only knew life in a cage. Among her many issues, she smelled bad and looked even worse. She was scared of us, and so we assumed she would be scared of the groomer but we had to give it a try. She went in for a bath and a nail trim and came out a diva with her head held high! We were shocked. Like humans, looking good actually made her feel good. These days her looks and personality make her a show-stopper! People see her as beautiful, but we see her as so much more! *–Jamie Burniston*

Ups and Downs: Annie has had challenges in her life. She was skinny and missing fur when I met her. She had calluses on her legs from life in a cage. Just as life was getting better, she ate four feet of string by pulling it from a beach towel and needed $1,400 emergency surgery (that was my challenge!). Regardless, she has been a best friend to my other Boston, Daisy, and a small, furry, four-legged blessing for me. *–Lisa Quintanar*

Cow Manure Connoisseur: As I sat on the floor of the foster home feeding treats to a terrified "Izzy," I just knew she was my girl. To my relief, a light bulb went on in her head when we adopted her, and she realized, "Wow! This is home and they love me!" It took no time at all for us to both prove each other right. Izzy may have failed as a breeding dog but she is the best farmhand I know. She patrols on the four-wheeler when she's not doing the "BT 500" around the house. Instead of hiding from me, she "muddies" me with affection after a good roll in the livestock tank – definitely my girl! *-Judy V.*

Buddy Come Home!

The Christmas my children, Chelsea and Logan, turned seven and eight, we agreed they could adopt a rescue dog. Naturally, we all went to meet our perspective friend to make sure he would be a perfect fit for our family. Buddy was enthusiastic and enjoyed playing with the kids as they romped on the floor, just like all the Boston Terriers I have known. Chelsea and Logan agreed they would share Buddy as their Christmas present, and we took him home.

Buddy was super friendly from day one and loved to visit with everyone in the neighborhood. Savannah, our adopted golden retriever mix took to him instantly. She was thrilled to have a "buddy" too.

My daughter Chelsea lived for this dog, making Buddy her favorite playmate. She dressed him up and even had a pretend wedding ceremony with him. He took it all with such joy—any game was good for him!

Buddy truly lived up to his name for the next four years until one day it all came crashing down. Buddy was gone. Living on the desert wash where many predators roamed, I feared the worst. But as wishful thinking on my part, I told the kids that he was probably fine and had just gone with another family.

We mourned his loss for a year and a half, and then I surprised the kids with another Boston puppy—again for Christmas. He was not from an adoption group and was very different from Buddy. He was extremely active and like a typical puppy, he survived on a diet of TV remotes and shoes!

Then one day, three years after Buddy disappeared, the phone rang. Buddy was at the pound! You can imagine how unbelievable it was. I kept saying, "ARE YOU KIDDING ME?!" Luckily, the kids were in school so I could rush down to the pound alone to make sure it really was Buddy. At the shelter I waited in line for them to get him from his kennel. It was an eternity...Was it Buddy? Would he remember me? Where had he been?

As it turns out, it was Buddy! Animal control had picked him up about 15 miles from our home. Even though he was thin, he didn't look like he had been living on the street. I personally think that someone from a landscaping crew picked him up all those years ago, and then either he ran away or the people just let him go. When the staff brought him out, he came straight to me and put his paw on my leg. I cried—I could not believe Buddy was in my arms again!

While he didn't look too bad, he turned out to be very sick with diarrhea and vomiting. My vet cleaned him up, and a few days later my daughter and I were able to bring him home. On the ride, Chelsea kept saying, "Can you believe he's back?"

When we got him home, even Savannah could hardly contain herself that her "buddy" was home again to play; she was so happy to see him. There was only one problem...now we had THREE dogs and two children, which was more than we could handle! It was a tough decision to decide who to get rid of (smirk!), but as luck would have it we never had to make the choice. It turned out that my brother was excited to have the "replacement" Boston come live with him! He had been begging us to do so almost since we first introduced them... so he finally got his wish, and he now has his own Boston too!

Buddy lived with us for two more years until cancer claimed his life. He should be a poster dog for having locator chips installed on your pets. It was only by scanning him that the shelter was able to find us, so without the chip this story would have had a very different ending.

We miss Buddy dearly and are glad we were able to have our "Lassie come home" moment with him, followed by two more great years.

 *Leslie Griffeth*

Fourth Time's the Charm

I never fancied myself a dog lover. When we inherited an older Boston Terrier named Jimmy upon my mother's passing I didn't really know what to do with him. Jimmy didn't like me very much, and I knew nothing about dogs.

It didn't take long, however, for me to find a soft spot in my heart for Jimmy. This poor guy was deaf, untrained and missed his mommy. My son fell completely in love with him, and we took it upon ourselves to teach him some sign language. He was a quick learner, even at his advanced age.

Unfortunately, just over a year after we "inherited" Jimmy, we lost him. At the age of twelve, he had an abscess on his eye, was blind, and his arthritis had progressed to the point where it immobilized him. His last few days were quite painful for him, and having to let him go was emotionally excruciating for me. I had become a dog person after all!

The agony of losing Jimmy was so intense that I thought I would never want another dog. However, after several months of missing the "tap, tap, tap, tap" of his paws across our floor, we were ready. I had never thought about how to acquire a dog, but I knew I wanted to adopt, not purchase one. I had seen too many ASPCA commercials to know that I didn't want to support a puppy mill by buying a dog at a pet store. This belief was reinforced by the "puppy mills exposed" episode of "Oprah" that I cried my way though. No way! I wanted to save a dog.

We looked at many, many, dogs online and seriously thought about rescuing for a few months. I initially wanted to adopt a French bulldog, but one was difficult to find. We also thought about adopting a Pit Bull, but we were used to a smaller breed. Ultimately, we decided to invite another Boston Terrier into our home.

We found MidAmerica Boston Terrier Rescue through Petfinder.com and started searching for our new family member. We filled out an application and spoke with two different foster moms before we decided on Gunnar, whose story touched our hearts.

Gunnar was initially bought from a breeder by another breeder, but that person never got his papers. Unable to breed him without papers, they sold him on Craigslist to an older couple. That couple found him to be too much of a handful, so they turned him over to a local rescue group. He was only one-and-a-half years old by then and had already experienced so many changes in his life. I wanted to love him, shelter him and show him what unconditional love was all about. His foster mom said he was playful and smart – just what we wanted!

Arranging to meet Gunnar was complicated because he was in Nebraska and we were in Minnesota. Eventually, we agreed to pick him up at another foster home that was about five hours away from our house. The first sight of him made the drive completely worthwhile... He was dressed in a sergeant major sweater and looked so cute! He was a little apprehensive at first, but after a few minutes of chit-chat, he was ready and willing to go with us. He sat on my lap during the ride home, and after a few hours of looking out the window and smelling us, he fell asleep.

The first two weeks were not easy. Gunnar pooped and peed in the house in the first minutes that we got him home. We quickly learned that whereas Jimmy had never needed kennel training and could easily roam the kitchen with the oldies station on for company when he was home alone, we could not do the same with Gunnar because our absence made him anxious. We would always return to a "present" on the floor. Gunnar also didn't like the next door neighbor's Boxer, Roxy. Jimmy always liked Roxy. It was obvious that this was a very different dog.

Despite these complications, we were completely in love, and so we decided to grit our teeth and stick with Gunnar. We were confident that, with patience and time, we could correct his undesirable behaviors.

I called the founder of the rescue group for assistance, who assured me that kenneling Gunnar while we were gone would make him feel safe and secure. She also told me to spray him with diluted lemon juice when he growled at Roxy or behaved badly inside. To our relief, these new techniques changed Gunnar's behavior for the better in only a few short weeks!

Now, almost five months later, Gunnar has fully adjusted. Accidents have been minimal and we no longer need to remind him about good behavior with lemon juice. He still doesn't like Roxy, but he likes our other neighbor's yellow Lab and Collie. I even took him on his first trip to the Fargo dog park recently, where he got along with everyone—dogs and people alike.

Though working with Gunnar was a bit of a struggle at first, I still believe that adopting him from a dog rescue group was a good decision. He has brought so much joy to our lives— who needs cereal to brighten your day when our dog chases the sunbeams breaking through the windows every morning? He comforts me when I feel low, and is a jogging buddy for my husband. Although it made me sad that he was so unwanted the first part of his life, I'm happy to know that he has found his forever home with a family who appreciates him.

 *Christina Patterson*

Love Will Conquer

I had two other Boston Terriers before rescuing Cricket. I fell in love with the breed with Murphy, then, I just had to get Delilah Mae. Despite coming from a reputable breeder, Delilah Mae has her own 'issues' and I feel I rescued her just in time!

I told myself, if I ever wanted to get 'just one more BT,' I would take in a rescue. We did, and the first few days in our home contained a new challenge—Cricket was dominant over the other two dogs and made no bones about it. She and Murphy got into a squabble where blood was drawn... Murphy's. Working with a behaviorist has helped, but we continue experiencing occasional horrifying, random outbursts, demonstrating the same Alpha aggressive behavior.

Regardless, I will not give up—this is not all her fault. I sometimes watch her as she sleeps, or while she chews on her toys, wondering. What happened to her must have been very traumatic. Only Cricket knows what triggers her anger. I can tell when the demons return to her mind, perhaps from life before she was placed with her with her angel foster mom, Barbara Carnahan. Quickly, we change the scene. I begin talking with her, stroking her gently, and the new Cricket comes back.

It's been almost a year and I still refuse to give up on her. Even though she doesn't snuggle like most Bostons do, there are many times in the course of the day that Cricket lets her guard down. It's then that I know there is a very loving baby inside, so eager to come out and stay out.

I love her so because she is Crickie, that little unique Boston Terrier that came into my life. Under her tough shell, in the quite times, she has such wonderment in her eyes they seem to dance. During those times I whisper in her ear, telling her how special she is, and that I will never leave her.

She is five yrs old, five years of meanness doesn't leave a heart so easily. But I won't give up on her.

 *Joyce Hayes*

One Dog's Gratitude

I must have died and gone to heaven, because this can't be real! All of these things happened so fast, and are so different from what I've know my whole life. I have a mom and dad who love me! My bed is soft, my food is warm and nourishing...and oh so many treats. All different colors and shapes! I have doggie clothes and a pink party collar with rosebuds on it!

After a lifetime of making babies, I've been told that I can finally take some time for myself. I didn't even know that there was such as thing; but now that I do, I'm pretty sure I LOVE it! It's hard to believe that only a year ago I was alone, in a rabbit crate, in a dark barn where no one paid any attention to me. That is, until it was time to make babies. No one petted me, and there were no walks or kisses. No one even talked to me!

I was rescued by a pretty young lady named Tiffany and taken to a vet for care. I don't even like to think about what a mess I was, with sores, patchy fur and missing teeth—the dog that went to the vet that day wasn't even me!

After a year the physical sores I had have healed and my fur has grown back in. Mom and dad didn't get me dentures, but I guess I can let that one slide... You know what's weird? I recently found out that I can do this thing they call "barking!" Who would have known that I could make noise? You should hear me now—not only do I talk, I can sing like a nightingale! I thought that noise was left to the squeaky rubber things my mom gives me, but now I know it's for me too! (On a side note, I'm not quite sure what to do with those squeaky things, but I like it when mom and dad squeeze them!)

Though I'm still not 100% sure about new people, I think my mom's ok because she pets me softly and says that I am very smart. How could I not trust someone who takes me for ice cream? She gives me baths, too! I sit in the water and get lathered with soap—it feels so good and I smell so pretty! Then I get to lounge in a soft towel that is warm from the dryer. It's times like that when I have to give myself a good scratch to remind myself that this is real!

Do you know that this lovely lady even bakes me chicken? The smell just drives me wild! Ah, life is good for me!! What more could I ever ask for? I have it all but I sometimes experience a twinge of guilt when I think of my brothers and sisters at the farm. Will they get to spend some time for themselves someday too?

 *Beanie*

(Translated by Helene and Leno Scarcia)

Who rescued who?

I am not a religious person, but I do have a deep faith in a higher power. This is a story of the universe connecting two dogs and one woman—all in need of rescuing.

Growing up a cowgirl in western South Dakota, our family's survival literally depended on the care our animals received. While we worked on the land with the cattle, our dogs were our constant companions. As odd as it may sound for a ranch, my first dog was a little Boston Terrier called Jiggs. He was at the ranch when I was born and became my guardian angel. I remember him playing with me, herding me out of danger and guarding my dreams at night. He passed away when I was about 12 years old but he remains in my heart forever.

By the time I was in my late twenties, I had a good job in education and owned a home; all I needed was another Boston. I looked seriously for almost a year, but something seemed to be stopping me. Then one day while I was at my parents' house, my dad saw an ad in the local paper for Boston puppies. My mom and I jumped in the pickup and went to look at them. Little did I know, this event would literally save my life.

When we arrived, the puppies tumbled out and the little, skinny, beat-up runt of the litter rushed right over and sat on my shoe, looking up at me as if to say "Glad you're here, where have you been? I'm ready to go!" I couldn't resist and Lulubelle immediately became my constant companion.

A few months later I was helping move a large herd of cattle on the ranch and my horse fell, causing me a serious brain injury. I had to relearn many verbal and motor skills. Having always been an athlete, cowgirl, and generally intelligent person, I felt like the brain injury had taken everything I knew about myself and turned it upside down. Those were dark days but the one light in the darkness was Lulubelle. No matter how bad my head hurt, or how tired and off-balance I was, she woke up every morning happy to see me and ready to go. Some days, taking care of Lulubelle was literally the only reason I could think of to get out of bed. Her constant happiness never failed to lift my spirits. Her boundless energy encouraged me to persevere through rehabilitation so that we could walk and play together. I truly believe she was meant to come into my life – I saved her from what could have ended up being a bad home, and she saved me during my brain injury rehabilitation.

A decade later I developed an almost overwhelming urge to have another Boston join my life. This time, I hoped to adopt an older dog, fearing a puppy would be too rambunctious for Lulubelle. Searching for the addition to our family, I became educated on puppy mills and rescue organizations. I found a Boston Terrier rescue group in my area and applied to adopt another female. Lo and behold, they called to say that they had a very special little male for adoption that was terrified of other male dogs, but loved females. Lulubelle and I took a leap of faith and Brady joined our family.

When I first saw Brady, he was so skinny you could count his ribs. Having spent his entire five-year life in a cage, he didn't understand stairs and didn't know how to play with toys. He couldn't even run around my yard without falling over. When something would scare him (almost everything scared him), he would run to a corner and hide his little face.

Six weeks after Brady arrived I had emergency surgery, and was basically confined to my house for two months. This turned out to be a real blessing. Brady received my constant attention and made leaps and bounds in his development. He gained confidence and learned the joy of running circles at top speed in our huge yard. Chasing toys and playing with Lulubelle was the most fun. Because of Brady, I had to get up and move-even when I didn't feel like it—which was critical to my recovery. He is now a confident, muscular little dog who thinks it is his calling in life to protect his "girls." These days I, too, have regained my strength; but I must admit that once again the rescue dog rescued the woman.

Brady and Lulubelle were meant to come into my life and to spend their lives with each other. It brings a smile to my face to watch them share a bed in front of the fireplace on cold Wyoming days. Because of their precious impact on my life, I pledge to make sure that every dog that joins my family in the future is a rescue, if for no other reason than to return the favor.

 Andrea Gilbert

A "Snort" Break

If It Looks Like a Duck... We adopted Dolly when she was a 12-week-old puppy. We were told that her parents were Bostons, she looked like a Boston and so we drew the logical conclusion that she was a Boston. A year later, if Dolly is any example, we've learned that just because "it looks like a duck and quacks like a duck" it doesn't mean it won't grow up to be an Ostrich! We love our 60lb "Boston Terrier" who has taught us never to assume... *–Donna Ronan*

It Sounds Good To Me: After an online search for a dog for my mother-in-law, I ended up with one of my own! Cooper's picture just stole my heart, but I didn't know at the time that he would also steal the show! It turns out that Cooper has a noteworthy enthusiasm for sound. Whether people are talking to him or it's just the television rambling on, Cooper is "listening intently!" To ensure that whoever is speaking knows that he cares, he nods his head in from side to side... again...and again...and again! He could listen for hours, but his talents don't stop there—he's also a wonderful singer! When the music starts a-rockin,' come on a-knockin'... Cooper's always ready for a sing-along! *–Denise Bays*

The Con Artist: Lucy becomes very quiet when she is not receiving my undivided attention. She leaves my side and instead makes a nest on my bed. When I go look for her, I find a Boston Terrier with the saddest, most dejected look on her face. Just as I try to pet or comfort her, she pulls her BALL out of a secret hiding place in her nest and runs off to entice me to play with her! *–Patty Corroon*

The Best Listener

When Jace came into the rescue group, he was thin and timid. His foster family helped him to put on some weight, and he quickly became a cute, fun-loving guy with an "attitude." When we met him for the first time, we were impressed with the way that he walked with an air of purpose and determination, as if he were on a mission.

Jace was relinquished by a family who found him too challenging. They couldn't handle both him and their new baby. The family said he was a handful, and perhaps not very smart. Upon surrendering him they complained that he just wouldn't listen.

When we heard about Jace through the rescue group, we simply couldn't resist! He was adorable, and it turns out that his previous family was wrong. It wasn't that he was stupid or a poor listener, the problem was that he was DEAF!

Since he came into our home, we have all learned sign language. To an outsider, the signs look very much like standard sign language, but we've simplified some of the hand signals to make learning easier for Jace. The signal is also accompanied by a verbal command. This way, our other Boston Bentley also learns the signals. Both dogs are now so familiar with the hand signs that we rarely bother with the verbal cues around the house. The signal for "no" sometimes has to be accompanied by a squirt from the water bottle (NEVER in the face) as a physical reminder that Jace is active in a behavior that is not allowed.

We have made up signs for my husband's name as well as mine, Jace's and Bentley's. We try to use them every time we talk to Jace about each other. When it's dark, we communicate with him through flashes from a laser pointer, or if he's in the yard, we flash the outside light as a signal for him to look at the door for his next command or simply come inside. When Jace is confused, he looks to Bentley for "listening" cues, and Bentley happily shows him what to do next.

We don't know if all deaf dogs are similar to Jace, but for him, being deaf is barely an inconvenience. We know that he is deaf, but sometimes we accuse him of faking...for a dog that can't hear something hit the floor, it's amazing how quickly he can find food that we drop!

Jace thrives on touch when you talk to him and likes to know where everyone is at all times. He'll regularly search the house to check on everyone's location and then go back to his resting spot. We have two older pugs that sleep downstairs, and often at night Jace will accompany them to their kennel so that he can see where they were going. He is a very loving, concerned companion and will not go to sleep at night until he knows that everyone is in his or her place.

One of Jace's favorite things to do is to climb into our laps and lean against our chests so that he can "have a talk" with us. His favorite person to "talk" to is my husband, Jerry, who makes Jace so content that he sometimes even falls asleep on him! Other naps are taken with Bentley, either in the afternoon or in front of the fire after a bath.

Jace's former family was right about one thing... he can be a bit of a handful during his waking hours! We've had to "Jace-proof" our home since he'll eat practically anything: buttons off baseball hats, paper from our printer... essentially anything that he can reach is fair game. Just as he keeps his mischievous eyes on us, we keep our eyes on him with a spray bottle close by, just in case...

Despite his occasional "sense of humor," Jace is very easy to love and has become a wonderful pet. "Talking" to Jace is sometimes difficult, but one thing is always clear: he never misunderstands a smile, and he always knows how to bring one out during a conversation!

 *Gerald and Leatha Pierce*

One-Eyed Handstand

Two older breeders from a puppy mill in upstate Pennsylvania, each blind in one eye, needed to be brought into rescue immediately or they were to be put down by the miller. My husband and I volunteered to foster one of the girls, and so we picked her up from a transport volunteer in Lancaster, PA. The nameless dog we were united with was extremely dirty and stinky, and was still wearing the FDA chains the puppy mill owner had on her little neck for the past eight years.

When we got her home, she was terrified to come out of the car. We cried as we put her in the grass for the first time because she was so scared, and clearly had no clue what to make of it. She stood there, unmoving, as if the grass were made of razor blades.

This dog was hurting. She had scars and marks on her legs and feet where she had slipped through her chicken wire cage at the mill. Her feet were swollen and torn, with splayed toes and bright red pads. Her ear was stuck back from being broken at some time, and her breath was terrible. She was so skinny that you could practically see all her bones, which creaked when she walked from being so cramped up for so long. Her eyes were cloudy blue—one with a huge scar, possibly what made her blind. We named her Ha-Na, which means "one" in Korean, since she could only see out of one eye.

Ha-Na was exhausted and constantly slept those first few days. It was clear that she needed to heal. We put homeopathic salve on her paws, and gave her antibiotics right away to help clear up her infections.

Ha-Na was afraid of everything. She cowered when we came near her, and curled up in a tight ball when we tried to pick her up. She hid in the back of her crate for almost a week before coming out to meet the other dogs and the rest of my family.

As soon as we could, my husband cut off her chains with a bolt cutter, which we've done for a few fosters in the past. The chains remind us of slavery and so removing them is always powerful and significant. For Ha-Na, it meant that finally, after eight years of breeding non-stop in that mill, she was free! Her neck was marked for a while, and I carried those chains with me for about a month, showing everyone I could. I still cry when I hold them in my hands.

We bathed the stinky girl and took her to the vet to get a thorough check up and appropriate vaccinations. Ha-Na was surprisingly healthy despite her physical appearance, which was new for us. Most of our prior mill dogs were sick and in need of some type of medical care. Ha-Na only had to have nine teeth extracted—on top of the 13 the vet said she was already missing. Interestingly, she went into heat about a week after coming to our home even though the miller gave her up because she would no longer breed. It was like she held it in so that she wouldn't have to stay at the mill. As soon as she got to our home, she let it out! Fortunately, Ha-Na had it a bit easier than some females we've rescued, I think because of her age.

Once the vet cleared Ha-Na, we introduced her to our four other female Bostons. Two of them are mill survivors, and they took to Ha-Na instantly. One became her best friend that day, and now they spend hours playing with each other. In fact, Ha-Na loves playing with all our dogs, which is a joy to see. Before we knew it, Ha-Na was learning how to be a dog! The yard became a happy place to trot around and go potty, and she quickly learned how to go up stairs and jump up onto the comfy couch. She took to my four-year-old right away, and she loves to give kisses to both dogs and humans. It seems Ha-Na has forgotten about the horrors of that mill and she has learned to trust us. She no longer cowers in fear or pees because she is afraid. She holds her head up and sticks her front teeth out as if she is saying, "I'm Ha-Na, aren't I pretty?"

Ha-Na has learned how to get around fairly well with her one good eye although she does occasionally bump into the walls or a toy left out on the floor. When that happens, she looks at it as if to say, "When did you get there?"

Full of fun, Ha-Na hides around corners, waits for her buddy to come by and then jumps out and tackles her! Always ready to put on a show, Ha-Na does handstands against the wall...honestly! She gets up on her front legs and puts her entire spine up against the wall in a handstand. She is actually scratching her back, but it has us in stitches every time! The other girls can't figure it out! She will do just about anything to get their attention. She will wait until the water bowl is empty, and as soon as the last drop of water is gone, she will run over to pick it up and then carry it around before putting it down in front of the other girls. I don't know if she is asking them to fill it up or just showing them that it is empty as if to say, "Can you believe mom hasn't filled it up yet?"

Ha-Na's favorite things are blankets, blankets and blankets. Those soft blankets comforted her creaky bones in her first days, and continue to provide the warmth and security she never had while living at the mill. She always has one with her, dragging it all around the house!

Time has healed Ha-Na's neck where the chains marked her, just as it has healed her spirit. Sadly for us, she is only our foster and not our "forever" dog. We would keep her if we could—she is a total sweetheart—but we need to keep the fifth spot open so that we can help the next mill "mom" when that urgent call from our rescue group comes.

 *Amy Angelo*

A "Snort" Break

Showered with Love: "When I first told my 73-year-old father that I was getting a Boston Terrier, he was mortified. He's not much of a dog person to begin with, and he's seen Boston Terriers on "America's Funniest Videos®" that always lick people on and in the mouth. That just disgusts him—and me too—to be honest. The day I brought Piglet home, I made a stop at my parents' for some reason. When I walked in the house, Piglet BOLTED straight for my dad who was relaxing in his recliner. She BOUNDED into his lap and licked his MOUTH! It was truly classic... 'America's Funniest®,' here we come! -*Erin Cox*

The Boston Tea Party: "I was going through a tough divorce and some scary medical issues when my daughter, Audrey, asked me for a dog. We ended up with Jack, who turned out to be the "little man" we needed in our lives. He often dons his "Sunday Best" (whatever Audrey stuffs him into) to attend her tea parties. She sits down and then he opens the door and prances in like a bunny; always eager to make her feel good with kisses and 'conversation.'" –*Nicole Valentine*

Boston on the Beat: While cattle dogs may be out working the fields, Pauley the Boston is patrolling the streets...in his golf cart! Day and night, Pauley keeps the peace on the course and in the neighborhood. He takes his job so seriously that he even insists on holding the keys on his collar. His specialty, you ask? "Cat" burglars! –*Alex Kenny*

The Devil Wears Fur

Ona sunny summer Saturday, I was teaching a little girl to swim while chatting to her grandma. I was telling her how I love dogs, and how much I wanted one, but was put off because I lived in an apartment. She told me to go check out a "fair" that a bunch of rescue societies where having later that day.

"At least you will get to play with them," is what she said...

Hiding my excitement, I convinced my unsuspecting husband to come "play" with the dogs with me. When we got there, I was in heaven, and my husband knew this was going to end up badly! I'd grown up with big dogs, so I went straight to the St. Bernard's, Weimaraner's and Collies; the dogs from my childhood.

As I glanced at the small dogs, I saw this little puppy, all nice and quiet, chewing on a toy and minding his own business. His face was half black and half white, and those beautiful big eyes, what sad eyes... I just could not stop looking at him, the cutest little dog! I then started asking the foster mom all kinds of questions. With each question I could see my husband looking at me thinking, "Oh no here we go!"

The puppy's name was Taz. I even joked, asking, "Taz? Hopefully not after the Tasmanian devil cartoon?"

The foster mom just laughed and said, "Of course not!"

She told me that Taz was found in Arkansas roaming the streets, most likely abandoned by a family, when the pound took him in and contacted the Boston recue. He was a bit on the skinny side but otherwise healthy. He got along fine with other dogs and had no problems with children.

On the drive home, I wanted that dog so badly that I kept looking at my husband with pleading eyes. To each of his concerns I had had a rational explanation or a great answer. I had it all figured out. By the time we reached home (30 minutes later) he said,

"Fine, go and find out what you need and we'll discuss it." If by "find out what you need," he meant, "find the address of the foster family," and by "we'll discuss it," he meant, "we'll go pick him up," then I followed his instructions to a "T." Since the foster parent had already spoken to us in person she had only a few more questions and to our huge surprise she handed Taz over to us right then and there.

All I could say was, "Oh no, we don't even have a leash!" We went straight to Petco to get supplies for Taz, while he went straight to a Bull Mastiff to play! I almost had a heart attack, but they were fine.

The reason for the name Taz became very apparent once we arrived home and the "devil" in him was released. The first thing he did was zoom around the whole apartment and leap, like Superman, onto the dining room table. Stunned, we stood back and watched as he flew all over his new home.

From the very beginning, Taz's life with us was full of turmoil. Neither my husband nor I knew much about the breed so when the "reverse sneezes" started happening I was on the phone with the rescue group, almost in tears, not knowing what was going on and in total panic! I found out this "reverse sneezing" is completely normal for dogs with short snouts. After several conversations, and a trip to the vet during that first week, I was at peace with the fact that Taz was simply experiencing allergies.

As the days turned into weeks, the three of us got to know each other and we began to feel that Taz had adopted us. He went from a skinny and seemingly sad dog to an amazing, bright-eyed companion. At first, Taz and my husband battled over who had the stronger will regarding training, but my husband took the lead (no pun intended), and with some patience, Taz learned a surprisingly vast array of tricks. He turned out to be very smart and even picked up on trying to "trick" us into thinking he did what he was told. For example, while learning to roll over, he would roll just his head -- instead of his whole body -- and then look for his treat with an expression that said, "What? Didn't you see it? It was great!"

It's a good thing that my husband and Taz bonded through training, because their affection for each other helped lessen the blow every time Taz ate one of my husband's Sports Illustrated® magazines. He's chewed up many things, but these magazines must be printed on gourmet paper because they are Taz' favorite "read."

Taz now puts most of his energy into serving as the "welcoming committee" whenever we are out walking. He "welcomes" joggers, walkers, bunnies, birds and even leaves! His best friend is a Newfoundland named Dewey who weighs in at about 150 lbs (compared to Taz' 20 lbs). They play "hide and seek" but Dewey doesn't need to go far to find Taz – he's hiding right underneath him! Even though he's always slimed when they are done, I'm glad that he made such a great friend.

Taz has proven to be an adorable, cute, and loyal dog, with A LOT of personality, and he knows how to play us: When he's caught doing something he shouldn't he knows it. His ears go back so far that they seem to cross each other and he looks at us with those beautiful brown eyes trying to hide the fact that he got caught. He pretends it was not him, and we can imagine him saying, "If I have this other toy in my mouth it couldn't have possibly been me that chewed up the mail!"

Our little man's antics bring us and all our neighbors so much joy that we almost look forward to these devilish times since they keep us on our toes. We may think we've taught Taz some tricks but he's always got one of his own to play on us.

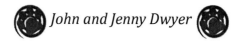 *John and Jenny Dwyer*

You Know What They Say About "Assume"

I moved to Santa Rosa last year to be with my fiancé Tim, leaving my Boston, Buster, with my father. They had bonded, and with my father's impending life-changing retirement, I didn't feel right taking Buster with me. So I packed up my Sheltie and left. I missed having a Bostie, so I talked to Tim about getting a puppy. I didn't know that there even were Bostie rescues! I assumed that since they are such expensive and in-demand dogs, there would never be any up for adoption—how naïve can one be? Anyway, I started an Internet search and came across "Bostons by the Bay Rescue" and Woofboard.com. I read all about rescue and how hard it can be for that 'right' dog to be placed in your home.

Due to Tim's job, we have things in our home that could be ruined due to leg lifting, so we really needed to stick to females. I applied, and we waited for our 'right' girl to find us. I had heard about Marlee, a five-month-old puppy who was surrendered to BBB. I really wanted her, but was told she was already spoken for. Oh well... There would be another, right?

Then, on Christmas Eve, I received an email saying Marlee was suddenly and sadly looking for a home and would we like her... I lost my mind, I was so excited! After an initial home visit, Marlee came to live with us on January 3rd. This was perfect timing for me as it was exactly one year since I'd lost my horse. I had raised Durk from a colt, shown him in competition, and spent many precious days out on the trails with him, enjoying the California countryside. He died following an emergency colic surgery, and it ripped my heart out.

Well, let me tell you, though Durk's death had been weighing on my mind, caring for an active five-month-old Boston didn't leave me much time to feel sorry for myself! Tim and I had our hands full 'round the clock. Marlee truly helped mend a broken heart.

Marlee is supermodel beautiful. We get MANY stunned comments about her being 'a rescue?' People always assume that her previous owner didn't know what she was getting into and made a bad choice. I tell them that her owner was an intelligent, sweet, older woman. She had bought this beautiful, registered dog with the best of intentions after losing her previous Boston Terrier to old age. Suddenly, her son and husband died, and her other dog developed medical issues, all putting her under emotional and financial strain. She found she didn't have the energy or emotion this darling puppy needed, so in desperation she sought help from her vet, who recommended adoption. Fortunately, I was given Marlee's former owner's contact information, which is not always appropriate in rescue, but in this case it was. I send her photos, and we've talked on the phone. Knowing Marlee is in a good home has helped her get through the devastating circumstances of Marlee's re-homing.

After adopting Marlee, we decided that we wanted another Boston. Daisy Mae had been picked up wandering the streets with a puppy at her side, and animal control took them both to the shelter. The cute puppy was adopted immediately, but Daisy was not so fortunate. She had displayed fear-aggression towards the shelter staff and since no one had claimed her, her options were not looking good at all. A GREAT foster home picked her up and devoted the next month and a half to getting her acclimated to other people and animals. Her foster mom took her to a huge dog park twice a day, which helped Daisy make friends and learn to trust humans again. Daisy was shy and had 'issues,' but she'd come a long way in a short period of time with her foster. We wanted to adopt her and agreed to a caveat; we'd employ training and behavior assistance to help her and Marlee thrive in a home together.

We met Daisy at the dog park with our other two dogs in tow. They all got along great, and after we spoke at length with the wonderful foster mom, we decided to give it a go.

Daisy is an unusual Boston; she has a tail and a bit of a nose. She is still shy, and sometimes when we walk through the house too fast or laugh a little too loud, she cowers. We know that with help, she will someday overcome her fears. In the meantime, she gives us more love in return than one could imagine, and she's a PERFECT 'big sister' to baby Marlee! When we rub her tummy and see the delight in her face, when she tosses toys in the air with Marlee, we can't imagine who would let her loose in the streets with a puppy.

The dogs' antics keep us laughing. When we're watching TV, they jump on the back of the couch and 'dive bomb' us, wanting our attention. Between the giggles, they get it... In the morning, they watch Tim tie his sneakers then, when he heads to the door, they 'attack' his feet, grab his laces and untie his shoes! We think it's because they don't want him to leave.

When we go to meet-ups and we are out and about, no one can believe our girls are rescues. People need to know that rescue groups take in emotionally damaged, troubled dogs as well as dogs from reputable breeders who have fallen on hard times. I've become a walking advertisement...I have a "Bostons By the Bay" t-shirt and when people ask about it, boy do they get an education!

There are many people who think the worst when they hear about rescue dogs. The contribution that our rescue dogs have made in our lives is a perfect example of how the contrary can be true. After meeting Marlee and Daisy Mae, people tend to have a change of heart, and they see that the best can happen to those who consider rescue.

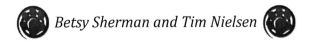 *Betsy Sherman and Tim Nielsen*

From Rags to Riches...to Rags...to Riches!

G inger is a doggie sausage who loves people enough to French kiss them all. She is our pride and joy... a sweet girl who loves watching her human brother and sister play soccer every weekend.

Ginger spent her early years as "Eva" and lived in a car with her "lady" and a puppy from her first litter. Her owner became homeless after losing her job and was left with no choice but to deal with this arrangement as best as she could.

Times were tough and to complicate things, little "Miss Eva" was now pregnant again. Eventually the decision had to be made to surrender the two dogs to a Boston Terrier rescue group in Nebraska.

In foster care, Eva had her second litter but nearly lost her life in the process. One of the puppies was stuck in the birth canal and after hours in labor, her foster mom rushed her to the vet where she underwent emergency surgery. Only one of her puppies survived and was appropriately named "Hope." Eva also survived and walked away with a nice little tummy tuck. What a life for a one-year-old.

Eva recovered wonderfully and was adopted by a family in Colorado. Her name was changed to "Ginger," but the turmoil in her life stayed the same. The family had no kids, no dogs, and no one stayed home with Ginger. Initially she was sick and weak from her surgery, but as she started feeling better her energy level turned up to high. Being left to her own devices, bored Ginger became quite destructive. Her frustrated owners tried to tame her with obedience lessons and very long walks, but these efforts appeared to energize Ginger further! She peed on the floor, chewed up shoes and climbed on tables to eat decorations. The family lived with this insanity for a year before giving Ginger back to the rescue group where she was fostered, coincidentally, by a good friend of my family.

At the time I wasn't even remotely in the market for the dog. I had recently lost my beloved dog "Hewie" rather traumatically and was a little gun shy. Truth be told, I was also tired of cleaning up POOP! Despite my resistance, and knowing the probable outcome, my husband still insisted we go meet the new arrival.

What was I to do? It was love at first sight! My kids loved her as she jumped all over them. She ran around the house, constantly returning to the kids and me. She was the cutest thing I had ever seen!

We did not take her home that night. I needed to think about it and told no one about my feelings until the next morning. As the sun came up and my husband and I lay in bed listening to the sound of my kids playing, I asked him, "What do you think?"

"Think about what?" he said.

"What do you think about Ginger? Should we adopt her?" I said.

Knowing how hurt I still was from our loss, it was kind that my husband allowed me the decision. Keeping silent was apparently very difficult for him because as soon as I asked, I saw his face light up and he answered with an enthusiastic "YES!" From there we decided that Ginger would be a combined birthday gift for my daughter and me since both our birthdays were that month. My gift was her front half, and my daughter's was the back (who do you think drew the short straw in that decision?). For at least a week I teased her by only letting her pet Ginger's rear! Oh, and NO POOP FOR ME!

As the weeks continued I found that I had no problem cleaning up after Ginger, and, in fact, was glad to do so. She never had an accident in my house, and after living with her for years, now I cannot believe she did any of the things for which she was blamed by her previous family. I think she was meant to be with us all along.

Ginger and I have been inseparable since she arrived. During the day when I work she is by my feet, and at night she is under the covers (which I swore would never happen). All she needed was to be spoiled rotten...and now she's a happy, healthy, well-behaved dog!

 *Stella Bickford*

More Identities than Secret Agents

I t took me three years of searching online to find the right Boston Terrier (or two) for our family. We weren't looking for the perfect dog(s), just waiting for the perfect fit. My patience paid off the day I spotted two mellow, unassuming Boston Terriers sisters and recognized them as the ones I had been waiting for.

A woman with a big, loving heart and familiarity with Boston Terriers originally rescued these nameless dogs from a puppy mill. She named them Stacy and Macy and had them spayed so they would never again be used as puppy machines.

Although the woman initially began housetraining them by letting them out every hour or two, she was soon diagnosed with cancer and was not able to keep up with this schedule. With her hospital stays and so forth, her dogs were not let out as frequently. They were fed and given water but their housetraining was neglected. Sadly, after a battling for a year, the woman passed away. Stacy and Macy were left with her husband who was unwell himself and unable to properly care for the half-trained dogs. Fortunately, the extended family suggested surrendering the dogs to a rescue group for re-homing, and off they went.

Upon entering the foster program, Stacy and Macy were renamed Minnie Mouse and Tootsie. They were skittish and quickly retreated to the laundry room at the slightest movement in the house. The sisters found comfort in each other, and stuck together like glue. While afraid of humans and new situations, they had absolutely no aggression and related well toward other dogs.

When I saw them online, they were being fostered in North Carolina and not yet ready for adoption. The profile said that when they were ready, they had to go together. I kept checking back until one day they became available, and even for out-of-state adoption (which is fairly unusual). It seemed like the posting was speaking directly to me as I was in Connecticut!

In writing the group, I started out hopeful, but was told that while the posting did say, "out of state," they hadn't really meant out of state...seven states away. They were thinking more like a state next door. Though usually not so bold, I was determined to change their minds—I knew these two sisters belonged in MY family. I continued to press my case to be allowed to adopt these beautiful, now four-year-old, Boston Terriers.

Eventually I was put in touch with a U. S. Marine who was the foster coordinator. I answered all of her questions and she answered mine. I photographed and emailed pictures of our house and yard and found a local rescue group to do a home inspection/evaluation to submit to the group in North Carolina. With my husband's support I continued to pester the group to let me adopt these dogs. Since the group had no other potential adopters, they FINALLY gave in and said, "Yes!" They even found a volunteer to drive the dogs most of the way to our house, seven states away!

Minnie Mouse and Tootsie turned out to be that long-awaited, perfect fit for our family. They took instantly to our Chihuahuas and cats, which was very important to us. Though they clearly feared people, we didn't take it personally as we knew their history going into this arrangement. Their aversion to us didn't frustrate us, but we were rather saddened to see the materialization of their wayward past up close.

The larger one, Tootsie, seemed to have born the brunt of whatever had befallen them in their past because she was the most skittish. The first time we really noticed this was when my husband picked up a yardstick to measure something, and terrified, she flattened herself on the floor. Both Tootsie and Minnie Mouse were very protective of each other—if we picked one up, the other would follow along closely, anxiously looking up. When we put her back onto the floor the other would carefully sniff her to see if she was all right.

Over the long run, we were more successful at comforting Minnie Mouse and Tootsie than we were at housetraining. This wasn't that big of a deal for us since our inherited Chihuahua wasn't so good in that area either. She was five when she came to live with us, and her previous owner never even tried to housetrain her. I didn't have a clue about how to train these older dogs, but knew I didn't want to crate train Minnie Mouse and Tootsie because they had already spent so much of their lives in cages at the puppy mill. We compromised by only allowing the dogs in carpeted areas of the house under supervision. Otherwise they were confined to our split-level home's uncarpeted kitchen and the entire downstairs floor; not such a bad space for them to roam, and we did not mind the easy cleanup of the wood and tile floors. However, we remained steadfast in trying to build their confidence.

"Minnie Mouse" didn't seem to be a good name for a timid dog in which we wanted to foster confidence. We considered "Spike," but ended up with names that were close to the ones they came with. After careful consideration, "Minnie Mouse" and "Tootsie" became "Minna" and "Dulcie."

Dulcie's name turned out to be appropriate since "dulce" means "sweet" in Spanish, and we quickly found that she liked apples. I gave her a tiny piece occasionally but on one occasion I gave her two pieces—which turned out to be a bad idea. She started panting heavily, pacing and breaking out in hives all over! It was night, the vet was closed and I didn't have any antihistamine on hand, so I looked in my dog homeopathy book and found two potential remedies. I gave her one and she improved somewhat. I followed with the second, which, fortunately, returned her to normal. After having a similar but lesser reaction to watermelon, we've learned to avoid fruit completely.

We quickly found that bonding experiences with Dulcie often revolved around saving her life! Once, while walking on a dock, clumsy Dulcie fell in the water and didn't look as if she could swim to shore in her panic. My husband jumped in to rescue her, forgetting to first divest himself of his wallet and cell phone which, of course, were toast after that. The event turned out to be worth the loss for my husband, since it reduced Dulcie's fear of men and strengthened the bond between them.

Now, five years later, Minna and Dulcie don't flinch as often and have grown to trust my husband and me. They are sweet, gentle dogs who play well with our cats and were good companions to our Chihuahuas through their last days. Though it took them many names and homes before they found the ones that fit, for both them and us it was worth the wait.

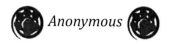 *Anonymous*

A "Snort" Break

Take One Dog and Call Me in the Morning: I was in my 70's, not in the best of health and slipping into depression from the loss of my wife. A doctor recommended I adopt a dog for companionship, and before I knew it, I was back on the road in my beloved RV with a tightly wound adventurer named Jiggs. Jiggs is now my copilot, traveling with me far and wide to great places like Yellowstone Park, the Grand Canyon and the Albuquerque Balloon Festival. He not only renewed my spirit, but also forced me to uphold a higher standard of cleanliness in our roving "home..." I couldn't help but clean up the dust-covered windows so that we could enjoy the wildlife and beauty our continent had to offer... together! -*"Steve" Stevens*

OW-de-le-ee-hoo! Toby had a botched neuter surgery two days before we picked him up. The poor guy was still bleeding from the huge incision and could barely walk. His pain was so fierce that he would lie on his back spread eagle in anticipation of the ice packs with which we consoled him. We found this to be a very strange excuse for a bonding experience... Our vet helped to get him back into shape, and after a challenging recovery, he has healed quite well. These days, he not only loves our nightly walks but demands them by spinning in circles and yodeling "Maaaaawm Maaaaawm" until I relent and off we go! –*Kerri Rivers*

Tough Love

I t all began with Macy, a Boston Terrier with a strong will and vigorous personality. At the age of five, she was diagnosed with a recurring mast cell tumor—a malignant and life-threatening cancer common to the breed. Typical of the Boston spirit, however, Macy healed beautifully after having her right rear leg amputated. Soon she was running, jumping and even catching rabbits. Macy recovered as though she never had all four legs; her fervor for life was unhampered.

Even as Macy thrived, I couldn't control my fear that despite Macy's favorable prognosis her genetics were against us. The same genes that caused the first tumor could potentially produce another one. In my mind, Macy's life was expiring, our time together fleeting. I grieved the impending loss of my beloved baby every day as I studied her face and tried to preserve as much of her in my memory as I could, only to find those memories collecting in a leaky bucket. After a year and a half of despair I decided that I needed a pup, ready and able to help me rebound should the unthinkable occur.

The profile of my new addition was this: a young female Boston Terrier, smaller than Macy's 16 pounds, gentle in nature and disinterested in rough canine play so as to not to bully my three-legged, seven-year-old angel. I thought that it would be tough to find a Boston fitting this description since the breed is typically high strung, 20-25 pounds, and the younger the pup the higher the energy level. Regardless, I persevered.

It took about three months of searching but I finally came across a dog that appeared to fit my desires. I saw her on the roster of available foster dogs at Boston Terrier Rescue of North Carolina. She was confiscated by authorities from a puppy mill in South Carolina where she had been tied to a tree with no shelter and used as a breeding dog. The description painted a picture of a shy and delicate girl, which would work well for Macy, so I grabbed the phone and made arrangements to adopt her.

I picked her up on a cold winter day from her loving foster mom in South Carolina. As I held her on the drive home and pondered a name for her, she curled her tiny black body into a ball as if trying to make herself disappear. I studied her sad eyes and furrowed brow, which told me that everything was big, unfamiliar and scary for her. She reminded me of a small sea creature just emerging from its shell after having spent its entire life in seclusion at the bottom of the ocean floor. She was a beautiful creation of nature—hidden, neglected and fragile. She was a little black "Pearl."

My first instinct was to treat Pearl with constant doting, kisses and labored goodbyes in the morning, just as I always did with Macy. Macy was confident, independent and housetrained, and easily entertained herself by playing only with her designated toys. Since they were both Boston Terriers, I had no reason to believe Pearl would be any different. However, Pearl quickly proved to me that kisses and doting would not be enough to help her leave her past behind.

The lasting impact of her traumatic puppyhood manifested itself in many ways and it broke my heart. During the evenings she stayed in a fetal position on the couch, looking as though she wished she could melt into the cushions. She refused to potty outside, and when I left for work, she destroyed anything she could get her mouth on, including shoes, the arms of chairs, the phone charger, my glasses, and, eventually electrical cords.

I knew that I had to do something to protect her from herself and quickly realized crate training would be the best option. The first two days in a wire crate were horrific. I came home to the crate partially dismantled and Pearl's forehead bleeding. Not knowing what else to do I consulted a dog trainer, who turned out to be exactly what we needed.

The trainer quickly taught me that love comes in a variety of forms and is truly defined by the perception of the recipient. He explained that a dog like Pearl needs a leader and, by kissing her and picking her up, I was showing her submission. She was already a lump of nerves, and my gestures were compounding her fears. He taught me that the way to pull her out of her slump was to show her that I was in charge and able to keep her safe. With Pearl I needed to learn to be the alpha.

I quickly made changes according to the trainer's instructions. I stopped carrying Pearl and instead gently led her outside on her leash. My gushing good-byes became a non-event (apparently making a big deal out of leaving was also triggering Pearl's anxiety), and I only praised her when she truly deserved it. One of the hardest things for me was to ignore her when she clearly wanted me to pick her up.

Most useful was the advice the trainer gave about crate training. He taught me that a combination of positive reinforcement and repetition could help turn Pearl's perspective on her crate from an undesirable place to a safe place. Additionally I learned that getting Pearl in and out of the crate should be done without fanfare to reinforce the idea that crating was no big deal. We switched from a wire to a plastic crate to keep Pearl from hurting herself, and then practiced having Pearl "kennel up" (enter the kennel) and "kennel out" (leave the kennel). The idea was that entering wouldn't be so traumatic if she was familiar with exiting after only seconds or minutes. I also started feeding her in her crate to reinforce the idea that the crate was a happy place.

A paragraph or two doesn't give justice to the work we did as it took a lot of time, patience and perseverance. After a week of very intensive focus I was uplifted to see the new training techniques paying off. Pearl stopped showing signs of distress inside the crate—no tossing her blankets or turning over her water bowl. Within two weeks she began entering the crate without being told. Crating kept her safe and secure while eliminating the destruction she had been causing. Within a month she was comfortably moving around the house when we were home, and the progress she made in her crate was amazing. She even started playing with toys!

These days Pearl is a happy, "whole" dog. She is still a bit skittish and clingy, but she has also learned love. She spends her days romping around with her best friend Macy, who, despite my fears, has showed no signs of genetic malfunction.

As for me, it turns out that my furry children are polar opposites even though they are of the same breed, which allows them to each uniquely contribute to my life. Macy is my "pickup truck." I rely on her and she never lets me down. Pearl is my "sports car." She's a luxury that brings joy into my life and I feel spoiled when I spend time with her. While Macy taught me about hope, Pearl taught me humility and patience. The difference between these look-alike dogs has somehow brought a new balance to my life that strengthens me wherever I go.

 *Dana Harrington*

A "Gotcha Day" Wish

I t was five years ago that we saw you for the first time. I still remember you looking at us from behind the backyard fence, head cocked with those huge ears. I knew right then we would be taking you home.

We may have saved you, Mr. Snicks, but you saved us, too. Our life is so much richer now that you are in our home.

The hours you play with your sister Georgia, and your little antics, melt our hearts. You are our shadow-dog, always having to be near us, seeing what we are doing. Never demanding, yet always eager for cuddles or belly rubs.

Many things about your former life we do not know. You came to us a little fearful and a lot thin. Your ears were infected and you had scabs on your head. You wouldn't give kisses at first, maybe it was frowned upon by your previous owners. All has been healed in the time you have been with us, no fear of kisses and you are definitely not thin anymore!!!

I was afraid at first I wouldn't be able to love you like I love our Georgia, but you wormed your way into my heart with your gentle manner. We love you more every day.

I'm sorry I don't know your birthday, Mr. Snicks. So instead, here's a "Gotcha Day" toast. "To my "old man" my "cuddle bug," my "Snickies," or "Snickerdoodle," thank you for coming to stay with us. Thank you for coming into our home and into our hearts. Our lives are better because of you.

 *Mary Hook-Goranson*

What is Rescue?

There are as many answers to that question as there are rescue groups. Some rescue groups are large; others have only one or two members. Some have shelter space to house the rescued pets, and others have members who open their homes to rescued dogs. Groups take in a variety of dogs: the young and healthy; the young and chronically ill; the young and handicapped; the old and healthy; the old with chronic health problems and the old with terminal conditions. The goal, of course, is to adopt them all out to "forever" homes. Some older and less healthy dogs are not best served by moving them from home to home so some rescues have a sanctuary program. In sanctuary, these dogs remain in rescue as they live out their lives.

My rescue group, Boston Terrier Rescue of North Carolina, was privileged to provide sanctuary to Adam, who crossed the Rainbow Bridge on March 12, 2009. Adam could be the poster boy for a very important aspect of rescue which is not often in the spotlight—dogs who deserve love and dignity to pass on.

There in a shelter, alone in a cage sat Adam. It was November of 2007, just before Thanksgiving. He was weak, very underweight, with no light in his eyes. We can only assume that since he was well into his teenage years, he once had a loving home and family. We will never know his past, which is part of the frustration of rescue.

It would have been a simple thing to walk by Adam's cage, say a silent prayer for his quick passing and move on. A rescuer, however, is not programmed for this. Instead, our volunteer looked at Adam and knew immediately she would take him home to die in warmth, blankets, good food, canine companionship and love. She was actually at the shelter for another dog, and the workers just happened to mention this pitiful senior. He was named Adam with a nod to Adam and Eve—the original! His life expectancy was about two weeks, but at least with our volunteer it would be two weeks not in a cage or on a cold shelter floor. Sometimes that has to be enough.

No one told Adam that he was only supposed to live for two weeks, and the spirit of a living being is often rejuvenated when basic needs are met. Adam relished in the comfort and safety of his new home. There were arms to hold him, hands to pet him, fresh water and food, treats, blankets and beds to choose. Adam decided that life was worth one more try.

For a year and a half Adam lived, not existed, but lived his life. He chose which furry friends to play with, which bed to sleep in, and steadfastly refused to enter his crate unless it was clean and smelled of Lysol. His caretaker, his "mom," happily complied.

In March, it was not Adam's spirit that failed him; it was the physical body in which the spirit resided that had given this world all it had. By this time, Adam had difficulty standing, staying erect, and walking. He accepted each new day as a gift, but was also confused as to why he could not stand and enjoy his water. It was the same love and care that caused our volunteer to take Adam home from the shelter that gave her the strength to guide Adam over the Bridge. Today, Adam lies beneath a rose bush in his Grandma's garden. This seems a much better end than alone in a cage.

Yes, our volunteer could have just walked by Adam's cage that November day, but instead she answered the question, "What is Rescue?"

 *Peggy Longenecker*

Training Challenges

Inseparable: As with many former puppy mill breeders, Kate was very nervous when we got her, and didn't know how to do stairs. Luckily, "big brother" John Henry was right there to lead her down and up. She was afraid to be petted, but again John Henry demonstrated how to enjoy it. He showed her the dog door, toys and our yard. In essence, having a well-socialized dog in the house significantly helped Kate adjust to her new surroundings and made our job very easy – all we had to do was wait and love. *–David Caldwell*

The Magic of Christmas: Dock lived in a puppy mill for the first three years of his life. When we got him he only shook and shivered. He would often run or cower, so we kept his leash on at all times. We didn't know what to do, so we tried total immersion... We took him to a Christmas Party! We knew it would either make or break him, but we had to give it a try. Turns out, it was just what he needed! We don't know if it was his Santa's Coat or the overwhelming amount of treats he surely received, but he confidently mingled and accepted love. From that point on he was not usually afraid – a true Christmas miracle! *– Angela Purinton*

I'll be Out in a Second: Some dogs do well in kennels—and, we discovered, some just don't. Unfortunately, Toby was one of the latter. He would poop in his kennel and then roll in it, which created a stinky mess to come home to every day! We tried some things like a softer cushion, which cut the pooping in half and significantly reduced the rolling. We also tried to occupy him with frozen peanut butter balls but Toby wasn't interested. Our last resort was to try NOT kenneling him, but this resulted in the conspicuous consumption of all things man-made. After too many frustrating months, we've finally worked out that Toby likes the bathroom! We can leave him in there with the light on, knowing that he's happy and safe. –*Kerri Rivers*

Big Help in Little Packages: Midge was our first adopted Boston Terrier. She was from a puppy mill and apparently didn't know how to bark or play. In fact, for the first few weeks we had her, we weren't even sure if she knew how to walk. She just sat, lifeless. Our hope for this little dog was turning to despair, until one glorious day Midge met our friend's Chinese Crested dog named "Nina" and everything finally changed in her life. Nina and our chubby Chihuahua, Toby, ran around our house like they were crazy, and Midge couldn't resist but to join in the fun! We were astonished, and broke out in a mixture of laughter and tears of joy. These little clowns just ran and tumbled around like children, and eventually we even heard a bark! It was Midge! She found her inner dog! Ever since that day, Midge is happy to run and play with the dogs and will greet folks at the door. She has become the happiest one in the house, and in turn, we now have the happiest house! –*Mary and Ron Seymour*

He's Just Not a Corn Dog: Poor Ralphie…his family wanted to get rid of him so badly that they faked that they were moving! When I went to pick him up I pretended not to notice the lack of moving boxes…what was I getting myself into? I quickly found out that I was knee deep in doodoo with my new dog… literally! Ralphie had a poopy problem! It wasn't that he didn't know he was supposed to go outside; it was that he just couldn't hold it. This was clearly embarrassing for him and of course, a mess for us! Fortunately, his problem turned out to require a simple solution – he was allergic to corn and additives! Once we switched to a natural dog food the problem went away within two days! –*Ruthann Hernandez*

A Boston's Favorite Treat

Have you ever cooked for your beloved Boston? Homemade entrees and treats offer cost savings and control over what goes into their bellies. Why not give this recipe a try? It's been Boston tested, and received two ears up!

Polly's Stroganoff

Number of Servings: 12 for small-to-medium Bostons, 6 for larger dogs

- 4 ounces leftover cooked beef, diced
- 4 ounce can mushrooms, drained and chopped
- 2 ½ cups medium egg noodles cooked according to the package directions
- ¼ cup frozen or fresh peas
- ¼ cup frozen sliced carrots, defrosted and diced
- 2 tablespoons vegetable oil
- 2 tablespoons flour
- 1 cup beef broth

In a large skillet over medium heat combine the beef, mushrooms, noodles, peas, and carrots. Cook and stir for about 5 minutes or until hot. Add oil and sprinkle with flour. Cook and stir constantly until the flour is incorporated. Cook one minute more. Slowly add the broth, stirring the whole time. Continue to cook and stir until sauce thickens. Remove from heat and cool. Put serving size portions into freezer bags and store in freezer. Defrost each portion in the refrigerator the day before serving. Microwave for 30 seconds before serving if desired.

From *Cooking with Polly – Culinary Adventures with a Boston Terrier* by Barbara Avery

To Love the Simple Things

Bibi, with wagging tail and Boston smile.

She came to me with wagging tail and Boston Smile.

Her first life—long, hard and a mystery.

Fresh sutures proclaimed her a baby-making machine no more!

Her skin dull and patchy, what cheap kibble did she eat?

Grayed muzzle said she'd done a lot of living,

But nothing said what that living was like.

She came to me with wagging tail and Boston smile.

Her first life over and a new life starting.

Good food! New toys! A brother! A mother!

Love wrapped around her like a warm baby blanket,

Hesitant and scared, she wondered what this was.

But she came to me with wagging tail and Boston smile.

"Eat fast! Don't share! How long will it be there?"

She ate so much she grew round as a cherry.

The doctor proclaimed her eyes a disaster,

Ulcers and tears, why were they neglected?

Didn't they see the love shining there?

But she came to me with wagging tail and Boston smile.

Why was she stiff as a board when picked up?

Was there a memory of once being dropped?

Why did she get nasty when brother tried to play?

Maybe no friends in the place she had been.

But that was then and this is now!

And she looks at me and wags her tail.

Back and Forth and Forth and Back.

The vet's office now a familiar place.

So quiet, so brave, never a bite or a whimper,

"Do what you must and I'll sit with no fuss."

Stingy eye drops and pills to swallow,

Surgery to heal the eyes that had seen such pain.

Sitting quiet. Ears held high.

She came to me with wagging tail and Boston smile.

As the months roll on, her trust grows and grows.

Annoying brother—now wrestling and tug-a-war partner.

"This play...this is new! What fun! I never knew!"

"Ok not to eat so fast or finish it all,

More will come—I believe it now."

"I came to her with wagging tail and Boston smile".

This last surgery to take care of small ills,

Comes back with a sentence of despair.

"Mommy cries and I don't know why.

I'm still happy. I'm still having fun."

"Didn't I come to her with wagging tail and great big smile"?

So—a lesson learned from this bundle of fur.

"Ok to love and play and try new things.

Tomorrow's not here,

So why should I fret?

There's food to eat and faces to kiss.

And if this time is short, that is OK.

Because I live it...

"...with wagging tail and Boston smile."

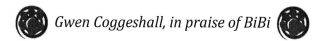 *Gwen Coggeshall, in praise of BiBi*

About Happy Tails Books™

Happy Tails Books™ was created to help support animal rescue efforts by showcasing the love, happiness and joy adopted dogs have to offer. With the help of animal rescue groups, stories are submitted by people who have adopted dogs, and then Happy Tails Books™ compiles them into breed (or type) specific books. These books serve not only to entertain, but also to educate readers about dog adoption and the characteristics of each specific type of dog. Happy Tails Books™ donates a portion of proceeds back to the rescue groups who help gather stories for the books.

 Happy Tails Books™

To submit a story or learn about other books Happy Tails Books™ publishes, please visit our website at http://happytailsbooks.com

We're Writing Books about ALL of Your Favorite Dogs!

Schnauzer Chihuahua Golden Retriever PUG

DACHSHUND German Shepherd Collie Boxer

Labrador Retriever Husky Beagle ALL AMERICAN

Border Collie Pit Bull Terrier Shih Tzu Miniature Pinscher

Chow Chow Australian Shephard Rottweiler Greyhound

Boston Terrier Jack Russell Poodle Cocker Spaniel

GREAT DANE Doberman Pinscher Yorkie SHEEPDOG

ST. BERNARD Pointer Blue Heeler

Find Them at Happytailsbooks.com!

Make your dog famous!

Do you have a great story about your adopted dog? We are looking for stories, poems and even your dog's favorite recipes to include on our website and in upcoming books! Please visit the website below for story guidelines and submission instructions! http://happytailsbooks.com/submit.htm